"...excellent communication skills required"

for Engineering Managers

Todd A. Shimoda

Published by
ASCE Press
American Society of Civil Engineers
345 East 47th Street
New York, New York 10017-2398

ABSTRACT

Todd Shimoda, in his book *"...excellent communication skills required" for Engineering Managers*, illustrates the communication process and presents techniques to improve written, spoken, and interpersonal communication skills. Since civil engineers must communicate with society, their ultimate employer, communication skills are necessary if they expect to be successful. Mr. Shimoda first presents the foundations of communication which involve understanding the communication models and the three communication principles of Topic, Audience, and Objective. Once he has laid these foundations, he presents specific guidelines to improving one's written, spoken, and interpersonal communication skills. With this publication, Todd Shimoda stresses that anyone can improve their communication skills if they understand the basic process of communication and practice the techniques.

Library of Congress Cataloging-in-Publication Data

Shimoda, Todd A.
    "...excellent communication skills required" for engineering managers / Todd A. Shimoda.
       p.   cm.
    Includes index.
    ISBN 0-7844-0047-4
    1. Communication in engineering. 2. Communication in management. I. Title.
    TA158.5.S45 1994   94-27491
    658.4'5—dc20   CIP

CONTENTS

ACKNOWLEDGMENTS

I wish to thank Zoe Foundotos, formerly with ASCE Press, and Joy E. Chau, Acquisitions Editor of ASCE Press, for their valuable help in developing this book. Thanks also to Linda Jaye Cox Shimoda for encouragement, suggestions, illustrations, photographs, and proofreading.

Chapter 1

INTRODUCTION

ENGINEERING

Civil Engineering Manager

Mid-size consulting firm needs
an outstanding engineer to
manage civil department. The
successful candidate will have
the following qualifications:
- professional registration
- ten years progressive
  experience
- BS in civil or related
  engineering
- MS or MBA preferred
- excellent communication skills
  required

Most employment ads for engineers and engineering managers are similar to the one shown. Along with education and experience, they nearly always mention "excellent communication skills required." In one major Sunday newspaper, over 75 percent of such ads mentioned "excellent communication skills" in one form or another such as:

- "excellent verbal ability"
- "must be able to write and speak well"
- "superior interpersonal skills"
- "must be a good communicator"

Why are communication skills emphasized for engineering and management positions? The answer to that question has two parts. One part is the very necessary reasons for communicating in the first place. The second is the vast amount of time spent communicating. Let's look at the time spent communicating first.

TIME SPENT COMMUNICATING

If you're an engineer, you might guess that at least half of your time involves communication: writing proposals, specifications, articles, manuals, reports, letters and memos; reading the same; giving presentations; or simply listening and talking. Your guess would be right, according to several studies. For example, Figure 1 illustrates the results of a survey of 1000 University of California at Berkeley engineering alumni.

Figure 1. An Engineer's Day (Data source: Zimmerman and Clark, 1987)

Monday	April 30
8:00	Writing
8:30	"
9:00	"
9:30	"
10:00	"
10:30	Reading
11:00	"
11:30	"
12:00	"
12:30	Lunch
1:00	"
1:30	Speaking
2:00	Engineering
2:30	"
3:00	"
3:30	"
4:00	"
4:30	"
5:00	

Other studies show that the time spent communicating increases with managerial and supervisory responsibility. In Figure 2, the numbers are for managers in general, not just engineering managers, but the trend is clear. Another interesting trend that can be seen is the shift from writing and reading to speaking and listening. Most speaking and listening occurs in meetings and in one-on-one (interpersonal) communication.

Figure 2. A Manager's Day (Data source: Walton, 1989)

```
Monday                                  April 30

 8:00    Listening
 8:30       "
 9:00       "
 9:30       "
10:00       "
10:30       "
11:00    Speaking
11:30       "
12:00       "
12:30       "
 1:00    Lunch (often more speaking
 1:30            and listening)
 2:00    Reading
 2:30       "
 3:00    Writing
 3:30       "
 4:00    Engineering or business
 4:30       "
 5:00
```

For the next few days, keep track of the time you spend communicating. You'll soon be convinced that the studies are right.

ENGINEERS AND COMMUNICATION

A common language is also a common way of thinking, which in turn largely defines a society. As societies become more complex, they increasingly depend on specialists who are increasingly knowledgeable in increasingly narrow fields. To make it all work, the specialists must be in constant communication. When communication fails, the bonds that hold together the functioning society, or at least pieces of it, can break.

Civil engineers ("civil" meaning in the employ of a society) wrestle with the problems of providing a livable and safe environment. The civil engineering profession reflects society's complexity and specialization. Civil engineers, in their quest to provide that livable and safe environment, cannot work in isolation. Not only must they communicate with other civil engineers and other specialists, they must communicate with society, their ultimate employer. To communicate is to be successful.

> Because the engineer's skill and judgment are sought
> out and scrutinized by a wide variety of constituents,
> from manufacturing experts to marketing experts to
> public interest groups and government, today's
> engineer must be able to speak and write clearly,
> precisely, and persuasively. (Whitman, 1991)

MANAGERS AND COMMUNICATION

Who do managers manage? People, of course. The only way to manage people is to communicate with them.

Engineering managers communicate with elected officials, government regulators, other engineers and scientists, technical support staff, clerical support staff, and members of the general public. Skillful management means communicating well with each of the groups, not just one.

If you're on your way up the corporate ladder, it's probably because you can communicate with a degree of proficiency. The more skillfully you communicate, the higher you can climb. The higher you climb, the more time you must dedicate to communication, and the more skillfully you must communicate.

> The ability to communicate and listen effectively is
> probably the most important skill at a manager's
> command, because all other management skills
> depend on it.
>
> *David P. Reynolds, chair of Reynolds Aluminum*

COMMUNICATION: ART, SCIENCE, OR BOTH?

Engineering curriculum concentrates on scientific theory and applications. The average engineering student takes a couple of English composition classes and maybe a public speaking course. These courses usually concentrate on style and composition issues from the rhetorical perspective. While the courses provide valuable knowledge, they often lack a solid scientific basis for improving communication skills. Engineers are highly trained scientific and analytical thinkers, why not apply those skills to communication?

The rhetorical method began with the Greek philosopher Aristotle over 23 centuries ago. Aristotle approached communication from the audience's perspective—that is, learning as much about them as possible and adjusting the message to fit their level of understanding. Rhetorical instruction focuses on the nuances of language, artfully composed. Aristotle's method is still used today, particularly in English composition programs.

With advances in social and psychological sciences, we have learned much about how we think, reason, and learn. Modern communication theory takes from those sciences, and others, and develops a more analytical approach to communication. In this book, both rhetoric and communication theory will be applied.

ACQUIRING EXCELLENT COMMUNICATION SKILLS

A word or two should be said about communication *skills*. A skill is a learned ability, rather than a gift or a natural talent. If you don't consider yourself a natural-born communicator, don't worry. There probably aren't any. Understanding the process and practicing, practicing, practicing will make anyone an excellent communicator.

This book illustrates the communication process and presents techniques to improve writing, speaking, and interpersonal skills. The book builds from one chapter to the next, so reading it in the order presented is a good idea. Also, the book is designed to be a quick reference that can be pulled from the shelf to solve a particular communication problem; or at least point you in the right direction.

Part I

THE FOUNDATIONS OF COMMUNICATION

Chapter 2

WHAT IS COMMUNICATION?

> The proper and immediate object of science is the acquirement, or communication, of truth.
>
> *Samuel Taylor Coleridge*

> What we've got here is a failure to communicate.
>
> *Cool Hand Luke*

Coleridge, the English poet and critic, neatly ties together science, truth, and communication. As he implies, the truth can only be acquired through communication. If truth is the goal of communication, then a failure to communicate can perpetuate untruths. And as Cool Hand Luke found out, shortly before the bullets started flying, that can be disastrous.

This chapter introduces a communication model, communication principles, and communication concepts. They will be applied to any form of communication, written or spoken or nonverbal. Before getting to that let's begin with a case study.

Wilted Lettuce and Urban Runoff

Eve Washington poked at her salad. She sighed. Another hotel luncheon.

Randall Martinez, seated next to her at the round table for eight, read Eve's name tag and said, "I hope you're enjoying the seminar more than the salad, Eve."

Eve forced a smile. "There's only one thing worse than iceberg lettuce. Wilted iceberg lettuce." She looked at his name tag, and held out her hand. "Nice to meet you, Randall."

He shook her hand and said, "The pleasure's mine."

How about you?" Eve asked. "Are you learning anything about urban runoff?"

He nodded and gracefully bit into an out-of-season cherry tomato. "Actually, yes. It's quite a good seminar. But the best thing is just being around other engineers. We speak the same language, if you know what I mean. Try explaining unit hydrographs to a group of homeowners and all you get is a blank stare."

Eve pushed her salad away uneaten. "I know exactly what you mean. And city council people are just as bad. And they're the ones who are supposed to be making informed decisions."

Randall nodded. "I agree. And have you noticed they'll rarely tell you they have no idea what you're talking about? They don't want the voters to find out how little they know."

Eve sipped her water, then said, "Exactly right."

Randall pointed to her salad with his fork, "Um, if you're not going to eat that ..."

COMMUNICATION MODEL

Eve and Randall seem to be communicating quite well, at least between themselves. Their mutual problem, as they found out, is communicating with those outside their profession. To help understand their problem and find a way to solve it, a simple model of the communication process will be developed in the following paragraphs.

Engineers make use of many models. Hydrologic models, groundwater models, structural models, traffic flow models are but a few. Constructed from laws of science and empirical data, models generalize reality. They allow engineers to more easily discuss specific situations and to predict outcomes. This communication model will have the same purpose.

The first question to answer in building the communication model is: Who is involved? In the case study, Eve and Randall described similar situations, each was trying to explain hydrology and hydraulics, or an application of hydrology and hydraulics, to a group of people. Essentially, two parties were involved: Eve or Randall, and the homeowners or city council members. In this case, Eve and Randall were sending information, while the others were receiving. As with all communication events, there are senders and receivers. Of course, most communication is two-way; that is, a sender can become a receiver, then return to sending.

The second question is: What exactly is the sender sending and the receiver receiving? Information, on the face of it. But as Eve and Randall found out, the information they thought they were sending wasn't being understood. Unfortunately, the homeowners and council members were receiving only noise. What the sender must send is *understanding*. The next step then is to substitute *understanding* for *information* in the model:

The third question is: Why wasn't the information sent being understood? Perhaps Eve and Randall were using the jargon or technical language of their profession. Perhaps the homeowners were so upset about having their property taxes raised to pay for the drainage improvements that they weren't really listening. Perhaps the poor room acoustics allowed them to hear only every other word. For whatever reason, if receivers can't understand the information, then they would be hearing, as said earlier, *noise*.

Figure 3. The RUN Communication Model

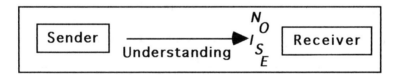

The key to the model is that for understanding to occur, noise must be reduced. And the first step in reducing noise is to identify it.

Noise can be the kind usually thought of, like static on a phone or too many people in a room talking at once. Noise also can be visual: unreadable copies, confusing graphs, poor page design. Language noise includes awkward sentences, inappropriate jargon, misspelled words. These kinds of noise and others will be elaborated on in the following chapters. The important thing to remember is that noise can creep in at all points of the communication process. To help receivers understand a message, noise must be reduced.

The communication model can easily be remembered as RUN (from receiver, understanding, noise). The RUN model will guide the remainder of this book's discussion. Incidentally, RUN was adapted from the communication model proposed by two Bell Laboratory engineers—Claude Shannon and Warren Weaver—in the late 1940s. Shannon and Weaver developed their model for use in electronic systems such as computers.

COMMUNICATION PRINCIPLES

In the discussion of models, engineering models were said to be based on laws or principles of science, such as the Laws of Thermodynamics. Likewise, RUN is based on three communication principles: the Topic Principle, the Audience Principle, and the Objective Principle. Each principle is introduced below; they are discussed in depth in the following chapters.

```
┌─────────────────────────────────────────────┐
│              Topic   Principle              │
│                                             │
│      Senders should be experts in what      │
│           they're communicating.            │
└─────────────────────────────────────────────┘
```

The more the sender knows about the topic, the more accurately and precisely the information can be communicated. The sender has more facts, which will help the sender meet the needs of the receivers.

```
┌─────────────────────────────────────────────┐
│            Audience   Principle             │
│                                             │
│   Senders should understand their audience, │
│            and meet their needs.            │
└─────────────────────────────────────────────┘
```

The more senders know about the audience receiving their communication, the better they can communicate understanding. Without such knowledge of the audience, senders have no basis for tailoring the message.

```
┌─────────────────────────────────────────────┐
│            Objective   Principle            │
│                                             │
│  Senders should know why they are communicating. │
└─────────────────────────────────────────────┘
```

Not many senders stop to think about why they are communicating in the first place. The Objective Principle constantly impacts the techniques and tips found in this book.

The three communication principles can easily be remembered by their initials: TAO. This initialism also spells the Chinese philosophy *Tao* (pronounced "dau"). Tao has many things to say about communication. For example, an underlying principle of Tao is polarity, which has a similar principle in the physical sciences: for every action there is an equal and opposite reaction. Applied to communication, the principle exhorts senders to carefully consider the effect of what they communicate.

Simplicity is another principle of Tao: Simplicity is elegance and elegance survives. Simplicity is also a theme that will constantly be repeated throughout this book. But be warned: simplicity does not mean the easy way. We've all seen a talented athlete who performs seemingly without effort. The athlete makes the triple flip or backhand look so easy. But if we try it ourselves, we quickly realize that hours and hours of training are required to achieve the same level.

Taoism

According to R. L. Wing (*The Tao of Power*), Tao means "the way the universe works." The word now refers to the philosophy composed in the 2500-year-old Chinese text *Tao Te Ching*, or "the classic text on achieving personal power through the order of the universe."

The author of the work, Lao Tzu, lived in the sixth century B.C. The work is a collection of 81 short passages. Lao Tzu was a keen observer of nature and the human mind. His passages reflect his observations in a way that can be applied in many situations, particularly in leading and managing people.

Lao Tzu's central message is that by understanding forces and patterns of the world, we don't have to fight against them to achieve our goals.

The following passage from the *Tao Te Ching* is particularly directed to skillful communication:

A good path has no ruts.
A good speech has no flaws.
A good analysis uses no schemes.

(From R. L. Wing, *The Tao of Power*)

OTHER COMMUNICATION CONCEPTS

Besides the communication model and principles, the following communication terms are used throughout this book:

- *Verbal communication.* In this book verbal communication means language, written or oral. In some senses of the word, verbal is synonymous with oral, as in *verbal commitment.* The terms *written* and *spoken* will be used to distinguish the two types of verbal communication.
- *Nonverbal communication.* Nonverbal communication is non-language communication and generally refers to gestures or body language.
- *Visual communication.* Visual communication is primarily printed, non-text based communication such as photos or illustrations.
- *Message.* A complete unit of communication. It can be made up of verbal, nonverbal, or visual communication, or any combination of the types of communication.
- *Channel.* The medium or media through which a message is sent.
- *Feedback.* A communicated reaction to a message.

SUMMARY

The communication model, principles, and concepts presented in this chapter give a consistent approach to communication. The RUN communication model identifies the three most important elements of the communication process: receiver, understanding, and noise. To send understanding, the sender must reduce noise that could muddle the message.

RUN was developed from the communication principles: topic, audience, and objective. As with RUN, TAO applies to any message, no matter through which channel it is delivered.

While Eve's and Randall's communication problems aren't solved yet, avenues have been identified that they can begin to explore.

Pass the salad dressing, please.

Chapter 3

TOPIC: WHAT WE COMMUNICATE

```
┌─────────────────────────────────────────┐
│              Topic   Principle            │
│                                           │
│   Senders should be experts in what they're │
│              communicating.               │
└─────────────────────────────────────────┘
```

Communication topics can be broad (for example, "transportation") or narrow ("roadway vertical curve design"). The trick is knowing when to send broadly defined knowledge and when to send narrowly defined knowledge.

Fortunately, this "trick" is easily learned: A sender has to know the topic the way an expert knows a topic. This chapter defines expert knowledge and also presents the three stages of becoming an expert, the typical topics communicated by engineers and managers, and the ethics of being an expert.

But first, let's examine the era in which we live: the so-called Information Age.

THE INFORMATION *OVERLOAD* AGE?

Each day, mega-billions of information bytes course through the arteries of computer chips, phone lines, satellite links, modems, and fax machines. Soon we will have 500 cable television channels. More magazines, books, and newsletters are being published than at any other time. Buzzwords include information super-highway, Ethernet, interface, network, multimedia, "fax me this-or-that," "I'm E-mailing you this-or-that," "let's do a teleconference," "leave me a voice mail," and so on.

Welcome to the Information Age—or should that be the Information *Overload* Age?

Whatever we call our times, it sure is getting noisy out there, isn't it? Maybe the Information Age needs a new name, a new theme, a new rallying point. Perhaps the communication model RUN gives a clue. *Understanding* was substituted for *information* because information by itself is benign, abstract, something you have to dig through to find what you want. What people really want, instead of mere information, is something they can understand. When they understand the information, they gain knowledge, which is what all of us really want.

Then how about calling our times the *Age of Knowledge*? The *Golden Age of Knowledge*? Well, that's a bit much. Perhaps the *Knowledge Age* will do. The first step in becoming a valued communicator in the Knowledge Age is to be a topic expert.

EXPERTS DEFINED

As already noted, society is becoming more complex, and to fit into the scheme of things each of us is becoming a specialist, an expert. Increasing specialization occurs because of the increasing knowledge generated by research and other energies devoted to any field of study. Specialization builds on itself: as we devote more time to a specialty, we become increasingly expert in that area, and the more we want to know about the topic. The following definition of an expert will be used in this book:

> A true and humble expert defines herself not by what
> she knows, but by what she knows she doesn't know.

In other words, a true expert has such an encompassing grasp on a topic that he (or she—gender-specific pronouns will be alternated in this book as discussed in Chapter 10) is aware of gaps or weak areas of his knowledge. A person beginning to learn a topic knows that he doesn't know much about the topic, but can't be more specific about what he doesn't know. He can't yet understand the topic-specific terminology, and certainly can't use it correctly. An expert in hydrology, for example, may know she doesn't know as much about groundwater hydrology as she does about surface-water hydrology. Yet a student just beginning to study hydrology may not know there's a difference.

And why the *humble* expert? Well, what creature is so despised as the self-proclaimed and loudly proclaiming expert? That creature doesn't communicate in tones of understanding, but at a screech that makes everyone want to run away. The quiet and humble expert's messages will ring loud and clear.

Another reason for being an expert is that it is easier to communicate understanding. The expert with her wealth of knowledge can communicate at different levels of detail. She can tailor her message for different audiences and objectives.

On the other hand, if approached incorrectly (not using the communication principles), then being an expert can make communication *more* difficult. The reason is that experts have so much more knowledge to communicate and they can trip over their vast knowledge getting from one thought to the next. Before discussing that in more detail, understanding how a person becomes an expert is useful. For most complex topics, we become experts in three stages.

The amateur stage. Knowing a little bit about a topic is usually pretty easy. All you have to do is read a couple of articles or books, do a couple of sample problems, watch an installation crew at work.

The competent stage. Reaching the next stage of knowledge requires an interest in the topic and a certain amount of study and practice. Reading more articles or books, getting down in the trenches, asking questions of experts, following the examples of experts, attending a few seminars and workshops, and applying the knowledge in some situations leads to the competent stage.

The expert stage. Knowing what you don't know, the sign of true experts, requires a deeper level of familiarity. Reaching this stage requires an exhaustive review of the available literature, attending more seminars and workshops, and applying that knowledge in many situations. You can now write technical articles, give presentations, or teach a course in the topic. You have now achieved a critical mass of accessible knowledge. And you know what is left to learn because a true and humble expert never stops learning. Congratulations and welcome to the expert stage.

SORTED KNOWLEDGE

Experts have accumulated a lot of topic knowledge and this alone helps with communication. But to communicate more skillfully, experts can do something much more valuable: they can sort their topic knowledge. When an expert tries to communicate a topic, she is immediately confronted (mentally) with all the bits of her interconnected knowledge.

Using unit hydrographs as an example, Figure 4 represents a few of the bits of knowledge and their connections related to the topic. The knowledge in this case is *unsorted*, and in fact is random and chaotic. You've probably experienced similar thought patterns when someone has asked you to explain a complex topic. You probably said or at least thought, "Where should I start?"

Figure 5 represents the same bits of knowledge, except they have been sorted into a more logical pattern. Which of the two figures is noisy? Which would be easier to use to write a report?

Figure 4. Unsorted Knowledge

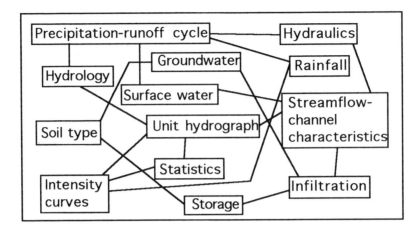

Figure 5. Sorted Knowledge

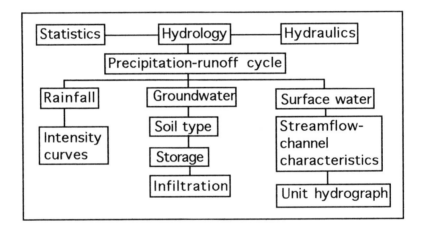

As you can see from the sorted knowledge illustration (Figure 5), the level of detail becomes more specialized going down the page. The direction from top to bottom represents how we usually learn a topic, from broad to specific.

The sorted knowledge approach can also be used to illustrate human knowledge structures, the ways our brains organize and retrieve information. There are billions of bits of information and links between them. Help out your brain, and the brains of receivers, by sending sorted-knowledge messages. Sorted knowledge points out any gaps in topic knowledge, provides a logical framework on which to target the message for the audience and objective, and generally helps messages flow smoothly.

The concept of sorted knowledge and human knowledge structures will be discussed in following chapters as the concept applies to other elements of the communication process.

ENGINEERING AND MANAGERIAL TOPICS

As an engineer, you primarily send and receive technical information. You write reports and give presentations in your area of expertise. The reports are usually the results of engineering analyses or studies.

The format of technical messages depends on the audience and the objective of the message. These will be discussed in the next chapters, as will specific applications to written and spoken messages. For now, remember that the best way to organize technical information to send understandable knowledge is through sorted knowledge.

Managers also communicate technical topics, but they also send many nontechnical messages. These nontechnical messages include business-related communications such as budget requests or thank you letters to clients. The Topic Principle applies to nontechnical messages as much as to technical topics. Be an expert. Know what you're talking about.

Of course, managers must not only communicate well themselves, but also must manage others' communication products. For technical products, such as drafted construction plans, you already know what makes a good product. First, the plans must be accurate. Second, the plans must meet certain drafting standards, either those of your organization or of the organization you're submitting them to. Third, they must be readable.

A manager must be able to similarly define the standards of the communication products because they define the quality of an organization as much as technical products. Examples of such standards will be given in later chapters.

ETHICS

Before we leave this chapter, a few words about being an ethical expert.

Knowledge is power.

Francis Bacon

So goes the old saying. Notice that it doesn't say that information is power. The saying also encompasses the reasons we must be ethical experts. The expert can decide which portion of his knowledge to communicate. An audience with less knowledge has to trust the expert to send correct and complete information. In this sense the expert is a knowledge "gatekeeper." The expert is constantly making choices on what to send. If the choices are not objective or do not tell the complete story then the sender may be unethical.

The ethical expert also admits there are gaps in her knowledge. She doesn't fake it, or deny the gaps exist. A simple "I'm not an expert in that area, but I'll find someone who is, or I'll get up to speed on it myself" works in most situations.

Remember our two engineers, Eve and Randall, eating lunch at the seminar on urban hydrology? (After the wilted-lettuce salad, they had creamed chicken something-or-other.) Their communication problem could also be considered an ethics problem. They didn't take that extra step, or few steps, to make their message understandable for the audience.

SUMMARY

The Topic Principle was the topic of this chapter. First, Information Age was changed to the Knowledge Age. Information by itself is benign; knowledge has worth. Experts have vast amounts of knowledge to communicate, but it must be sorted to allow effective communication.

> We consider her no-double-talk reports the only information we can trust about the project.
>
> *Members of the Denver City Council speaking about the engineer in charge of construction at the $3.5 billion Denver International Airport*

Chapter 4

AUDIENCE: THE FOCUS OF COMMUNICATION

```
Audience   Principle

Senders should understand their audience, and meet
                their needs.
```

Now that we're topic experts, we need to focus the sorted knowledge into an understandable message. The second communication principle will help us do that. Of the three TAO principles, the Audience Principle is arguably the most important.

This chapter discusses audience characteristics and gives specific examples of the audiences that engineers and managers frequently encounter. Also presented are pointers on analyzing and communicating effectively with those audiences. In addition, the chapter shows how to use feedback in the communication process.

FRAME OF REFERENCE AND UNDERSTANDING

Each person brings unique experiences, knowledge, and emotions to a communication setting. The sum of a person's unique experiences, knowledge, and emotions can be considered that person's frame of reference. A frame of reference allows a person to interpret, or ignore, a message. The more the sender's frame of reference is similar to that of the receiver, the easier it is to communicate understanding. Eve and Randall mentioned this, in different words, over their lunch. Figure 6 shows this visually.

The overlapping areas in Figure 6 indicate common knowledge areas in their frames of references. Obviously, Eve and Randall overlap more than Eve and the homeowner, at least for engineering topics. In Figure 7, some of the bits of knowledge of urban hydrology developed in the previous chapter have been inserted as well as the homeowner's limited knowledge of urban runoff to show how they might overlap.

Figure 6. Frames of Reference

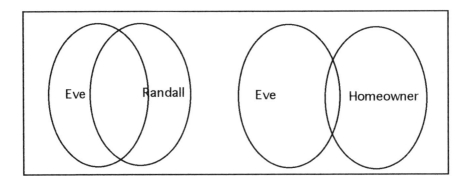

Figure 7. Specific Topic Knowledge Overlap

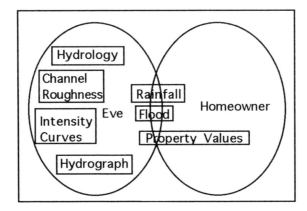

We need not be intimidated by limited overlapping frames of reference. Rather, we can take advantage of what overlap there is. Using common experiences and knowledge in communication is an easy way to facilitate understanding. The more we know about the receiver's frame of reference and knowledge structures, the more we can develop appropriate messages.

Okay, you buy the idea. Next we need to learn how to determine the audience's topic knowledge.

AUDIENCE ANALYSIS

Audience analysis is a burgeoning field of communication science. The field incorporates theory and application from diverse fields such as psychology, sociology, and marketing and advertising. Techniques include surveys, experiments, and focus groups. Obviously, the more at stake, the more effort understanding an audience should involve. Writing a proposal for a $10 million contract for engineering services should include the step of a detailed and written audience analysis. A one-page memo (no memo should be more than one page) to your boss doesn't require a detailed and written audience analysis, but still requires some thought about the audience (depending on the boss, of course; yours may be beyond analysis).

Never skip the step of trying to understand your audience.

Okay, you're not going to conduct a psychological experiment to find out the inner workings of your client, your boss, the city council member, or the home-owner trying to understand storm-water detention. But knowing a few general characteristics will allow you to go a long way to understanding your audience. These characteristic have been divided into the major categories of demographics, needs, and expectations.

Audience Demographics
- *Education and experience*. Both are in general terms, not necessarily specific to the topic. Knowing an audience's education and experience will allow you to use examples and analogies that will make sense to them.
- *Knowledge of the topic*. Here we are looking specifically at the audience's knowledge of the topic. Be sure to consider their understanding of the terminology peculiar to the topic.
- *Cultural background*. An audience's cultural background can be both societal and organizational. Societal culture is their personal environment and background, while organizational culture is their company or agency. Of course, societal and organizational culture can overlap.

Audience Needs
- *Knowledge*. Your audience isn't looking for information, but wants to increase their knowledge. They don't need to find out how much you know. They need the facts from you, the expert.
- *Understanding*. Your audience needs to understand the facts and concepts presented to them.

Audience Expectations
- *Conciseness*. We're all busier than ever. You need to determine how much time an audience is willing to give you.

- *Interest*. Your audience would like your message to be interesting and hold their attention. Tap into the audience's interests to keep your message riveting.

COMMUNICATING WITH SPECIFIC AUDIENCES

Engineers communicate with many categories of audiences. For example:
- Engineers with the same area of expertise
- Engineers in other areas of expertise
- Professionals in technical areas (architects, chemists, biologists)
- Professionals in nontechnical areas (attorneys, accountants)
- Technical support (surveyors, draftspersons, word processors)
- Trade support (contractors)
- Nontechnically oriented people (clients, the public)

Of course, managers communicate with the same audiences as engineers, but when in a managerial role, the categories often change. For example:
- Engineering managers at your level
- Engineering managers or directors above you
- Engineers under your supervision
- Technical support under your supervision
- Nontechnical support under your supervision
- Other employees in your organization
- Clients and customers
- Regulatory officials
- Elected officials
- General public

With each of the categories, the audience demographics, needs, and expectations can be determined. As an example, consider our two urban hydrologists, Eve and Randall. Let's assume they will be giving a presentation to a city council with the following members:
- Political science professor
- State agency biologist
- Car dealership owner
- Banking manager
- Small clothing store owner

The five members of the council are quite diverse, and Eve and Randall must consider each when preparing their presentation. Note that the list only mentions the council members' professions and doesn't include for example, their political affiliation, their stand on environmental or fiscal issues, or their past voting record. However, even this information should give Eve and Randall an idea of the frame of reference overlap, or lack of overlap, of their audience. It also gives them an idea of the audience's interests.

For example, the wildlife biologist will no doubt have the most knowledge about the topic since it is an environmental issue to a certain degree. For their presentation, Eve and Randall will have to study the biological ramifications of treating storm water. The small business owners will probably be most concerned about the costs to businesses for improvements or restrictions. The banking manager will also be closely following the economic issues. The political science professor will be considering the effects of past environmental legislation. Eve and Randall should include all these issues in their presentation. They should also realize that the most technical terminology will be beyond their audience's grasp.

Of course, most presentations to city councils are public, and the public will have a chance to comment. The audience analysis for this group is even more difficult because of the wide range of education and experiences. The following rule is good for general public presentations: For most general public presentations, assume that the audience knows nothing about your topic. But don't insult anyone's intelligence or be condescending.

USING FEEDBACK

Before you send out your report or give your presentation, leave time to have someone else read or listen to it. That someone should be in your targeted audience, or at least familiar with them. Ask your reviewer to note any areas that are confusing, not understandable, irrelevant, or boring. Be sure to tell your reviewer to be honest. Evaluate the criticism and adjust your communication products where necessary.

During a spoken presentation, always tell the audience they can ask for clarification during the presentation. That way you can make sure you are complying with the Audience Principle. You should also be sensitive to nonverbal feedback, such as puzzled looks or yawns. Skillful communicators can adjust on the fly; tips on doing this will be given in a later chapter.

SUMMARY

This chapter discussed the second, and perhaps most important, communication principle: The Audience Principle. The concept of frame of reference and overlapping knowledge structures was illustrated and examples of specific audiences were given. Using feedback to improve audience rapport was also discussed. The important thing to take away from this chapter is that skillful communicators are sensitive to their audience.

Chapter 5

OBJECTIVE: WHY WE COMMUNICATE

Objective   Principle
Senders should know why they are communicating.

The final communication principle, the Objective Principle, helps senders focus their messages even further. This chapter starts with a look at why communication objectives are important to skillful communication. Typical objectives for engineers and managers are discussed as well. The rest of the chapter shows how to combine the TAO principles and gives tips on message design choices such as channel, style, and tone.

IMPORTANCE OF COMMUNICATION OBJECTIVES

Unfortunately, we all know people who talk just to hear their own voice. What they say has little to do with the matter at hand. They never want you to join in the conversation, nor do they seem to care if you're even listening. They don't seem to have any constructive reason for talking. Their reports and memos ramble on and on, jumping from topic to topic without a clear destination.

The skillful communicator has a constructive reason, an objective, for speaking or writing. Having an objective allows the skillful communicator to tailor messages so they will be effective. Knowing the objective also helps communicators eliminate noise in their messages. Objectives allow their messages to be concise, keep on track, and accomplish something.

And win their audience's appreciation.

OBJECTIVES FOR ENGINEERS AND MANAGERS

In this section, the classic categories of communication objectives are defined. Communication researchers and specialists have applied various names for these categories, but the names used in this chapter are as follows:

- Inform (preferred: Increase Knowledge)
- Persuade
- Instruct
- Document

These objectives are the desired outcomes of a particular communication. Of course, the objectives may be present in any combination in a message, and the message may have to be adjusted when the objective changes.

Notice that none of the objectives is "Show how much the sender knows." That objective is only appropriate when the sender is being tested, as when they were in school. Unfortunately, that is precisely how we learned to communicate, especially to write. If there is one thing less skillful communicators can do to improve their skills, it is to remember that most communication is not to show how much they know.

Skillful communication means focusing a message to achieve a specific objective. The following paragraphs briefly introduce these communication objectives. Specific techniques that can be used to achieve the objectives will be presented in later chapters.

Increase Knowledge

Increase knowledge is preferred to *inform* for the same reason the Information Age was renamed the Knowledge Age. To simply inform an audience of a topic doesn't mean they will retain your message and be able to recall it later. To increase an audience's knowledge means that you've permanently increased or reinforced their knowledge structures for the topic. A few examples of communications that increase knowledge are as follows:

- Research reports
- Project or monthly status reports
- Seminar presentations

The following tips will help you craft messages that an audience can easily recall:

Sorted knowledge. The chapter on the Topic Principle showed that good communicators can sort their knowledge. Sorted knowledge allows messages to be presented logically, rather than as whim strikes. A message presented in a sorted, logical order allows the receivers to spend their mental energy increasing their knowledge rather than sorting the information themselves.

Message structure. Various message structures can help audiences increase their knowledge and recall. The general rule is that well-structured messages flow logically. For example, using a step-by-step approach like that used in a how-to guide gives receivers an easy-to-recall structure.

Messages that are presented in "chunks" are easier to recall. A chunk can be thought of as a subdivision of a message, such as a concept, step, example, chapter, paragraph, list item, and so on. The theory that chunks are easier to recall comes from short-term-memory studies. Research shows that we can hold about four to seven chunks of information in short-term memory before being processed into long-term memory or forgotten. For example, you would more easily remember a phone number that had the year of your birth in it: 555-1955. The last four digits form a chunk; you don't have to remember them individually. And the first three digits of the phone number are also easy to remember as a chunk. Therefore, the seven digit phone number has only two chunks to recall.

Another easy-to-recall message structure is the narrative, or stories. Stories are easy to remember because we're familiar with their form; we grew up on stories. The narrative form is essentially the unfolding of events over time. The case study involving Eve and Randall is an example of the narrative form.

Interest. An interesting message holds a receiver's attention. You can make a message interesting in many ways, but the main categories are personal interest and universal interest. Personal interest is something that interests you or your audience that may not interest someone else. For example, a story about golf will probably interest only those who golf. On the other hand, a story about someone winning a million dollars by hitting a hole-in-one would grab nearly everyone's attention.

Persuade

Much of our communication time is spent trying to persuade our audience. Persuade them to do what? Well, for example, to accept our point of view, to believe in the importance of our message, or to accept our proposal.

Persuasion involves three main steps:
- *Establish credibility.* Being an expert in the topic, as defined in Chapter 3, will help establish credibility. If your audience does not know who you are, then a brief introduction is in order.
- *Present facts.* People want to hear evidence rather than opinions.
- *Overcome any negatives with positives.* People usually bring preconceived opinions, which may or may not be based on facts, to a communication setting. You have to deal with negative opinions up front, rather than ignore them.

Instruct

When we instruct with our messages, we need to present the information in a step-by-step procedure. Examples of instruction include user documentation, operator's manuals, how-to guides, and office procedures.

The first two communication principles are important for instructional messages. The knowledge required to develop a step-by-step procedure must be complete; you can't leave out a step if you don't know enough about it. Also, knowing the audience is critical because you will need to know where to start in the procedure. Does your audience need background knowledge on the equipment? Do they need to know how to turn it on and off? Or do they need advanced programming instructions?

Document

In engineering, we often record what was done or said. A construction manager's diary is a good example. Meeting minutes are another example. These document-type messages are often used when a question arises as to what occurred.

The document message doesn't depend as much on Topic or Audience considerations as other types of messages. We often don't know who will be reading the document and for what purpose. The key is to be complete, clear, and concise.

COMBINING TOPIC, AUDIENCE, AND OBJECTIVE

Solving a communication problem is the same as solving an engineering problem. More than anything else, engineers are trained to be problem solvers. The steps in solving a problem can be generalized into the following steps:

1. Ask the right question. This is the key to problem solving. The right question is specific and complete.
2. Determine what method to use. The method can be an equation or series of equations, or which computer model to use. For a communication problem, the method could be that presented in this book.
3. List the data or knowledge you need to solve the problem.
4. List the data or knowledge you already have.
5. Find the data or knowledge you need.
6. Solve the problem.
7. Evaluate the solution.

You will no doubt be able to relate the steps to an engineering problem, such as an urban runoff problem. The simple example in Table 1 illustrates the process for communication:

Table 1. Problem-Solving Example

Step	Urban Runoff	Communication
1. Ask question	Peak runoff (100-yr storm) from new shopping center	Convince council to require detention and filtration ponds
2. Determine method	Rational method	TAO, RUN model
3. List data needed	Overland runoff coefficient, rainfall intensity for design storm, area	Topic: potential environmental damage Audience: who will be making decision? Objective: persuasion
4. List data have	Area, estimated paved and landscaped surfaces	Topic: increase in cfs Objective: know costs and negatives
5. Gather data needed	Intensity curves	Audience: council member profiles
6. Solve problem	55 cfs	Prepare presentation with benefits/costs
7. Evaluate solution	Reasonable, increased from 10 cfs undeveloped	Covers potential concerns, watch use of technical jargon

MESSAGE DESIGN CHOICES

Before leaving this part of the book, three important communication concepts will be introduced. They will be used in the discussion on the design of written and spoken messages. These concepts can be thought of as additional variables in solving a communication problem.

Channel choice. We have many more choices today mainly because the technology has come down in price to be accessible by nearly everyone. Most word processing programs are as sophisticated as desktop publishing programs were a few years ago. Color scanners and printers for sophisticated graphics are available to most companies. Inexpensive camcorders can produce quality videos. Most computers are now multimedia, which integrates digital sound, graphics, animation, video, and text.

So how do we choose a channel? When is text better than a graphic better than a video better than a multimedia presentation? That question is difficult to answer because the number of combinations is many. The choice certainly has a lot to do with the TAO communication principles. Some topics lend themselves better to a visual over a written presentation. The audience characteristics and the objective of the message also enter into the decision. Cost and time and expertise are other considerations.

Style. Style refers to the choices you have in designing your messages. The design choices include such details as page layout, font family, use of company logo, terminology used, proposal presentation style, abbreviations, and spelling. There are many others of course. You may have heard of books such as *The Chicago Manual of Style*. These references provide standards for document production. Many organizations develop their own style guides to provide consistency to their communication products.

As with channel choices, we have to be careful with style choices. Just because we can use color, for example, doesn't necessarily mean that we should use color in everything we do. And there are correct colors and color combinations to use. The same applies to fonts or typefaces. Word processing packages come with dozens of fonts to use. The temptation is to use as many as can fit on one page.

Tone. Communication tone refers to the way language is used to convey a message. Tone can be straightforward and serious, or light and friendly, or energetic, or quiet.

Again, the tone used depends on the TAO principles. However, the main goal of tone is to create interest. An interesting message holds the receiver's attention. The skillful communicator varies the tone so the audience can't go to sleep or daydream.

SUMMARY

This chapter on the Objective Principle showed the importance of knowing why we are communicating. Without determining our objective beforehand, we often don't say much of value to our audience. The four main types of objectives were presented along with examples of each. To end the first part of the book, the three TAO principles were tied together with an analogy to engineering problem solving. Lastly, three message design variables—channel choice, style, and tone—were introduced.

Now, on to the specifics of written messages.

Part II

WRITTEN COMMUNICATIONS

Chapter 6

BASICS OF WRITTEN MESSAGES

> Writing really stresses me out.
>
> *Civil engineer*

Writing—a dreaded word to many of us. Writing takes too much time and energy, and it never comes out as we want. But writing is a necessary part of engineering and management.

In this part of the book, a straightforward method of planning and developing good written messages is presented. Each chapter has several examples of writing, both good and not so good. In this first chapter on written messages, the basics of good writing are introduced. This chapter presents the categories of written messages, looks at the noise common to written messages, and attacks the myth of writer's block.

Before getting to that, let's see if we can figure out why writing can be so stressful.

THE DIFFICULTY OF WRITING

First, we learn to communicate by speaking. It's the most natural way to communicate and our brains are wired for speech communication. We don't learn written communication until after we've been speaking for several years. And while we learn to speak by listening and experimenting, we learn to write by being given sets of rules that don't lend themselves well to experimenting.

Second, writing is a very precise means of communication. Rules of grammar and syntax can intimidate us. When we speak, we are less encumbered by those rules; we use them, for sure, but we use them more naturally, without conscious thought.

Third, when we are speaking we usually get instant feedback. We know when we have to backtrack and explain terms that aren't being understood. We know what the audience feels is important by the questions they ask. Writing is much more solitary, and we have to anticipate feedback.

Finally (although there may be other reasons), writing is just plain no fun. While solving an engineering problem often involves dozens of variables and differential equations; writing a complex report involves many times more variables (ideas, words, sentences, paragraphs, grammar). Writing takes massive cognitive effort; it requires focusing all of our mental abilities. Professional writers often dread sitting down in front of the keyboard.

Well, I hope I haven't scared you off. The point is that there are reasons why writing can be stressful. If we know the reasons we can work to overcome them. The rest of this chapter, as well as this part of the book, will break up the difficult process into smaller tasks that can be taken one at a time.

Writing may never be loads of fun, but it can be less dreaded.

CATEGORIES OF WRITTEN MESSAGES

The categories of written messages presented in this section have been divided into technical and business messages, although they often overlap. The details of constructing specific written messages will be discussed in the following chapters. In general, written messages are preferred for permanent records because they are a very precise form of communication. Written messages are usually the most cost-effective way to send a lot of information to many receivers.

Technical Messages

The topics of technical written messages are those in which a sender is expert. The audiences can range from other experts to those who know nothing about the topic. Likewise, the objectives can be any of the four: increase knowledge, persuade, instruct, or document. The following are the most common examples of technical messages:

- *Reports.* Technical reports usually document the results of a study or an engineering analysis. The objective is also to increase knowledge about the topic. Audience considerations are important: the less expert the audience in the topic, the more background knowledge a sender must provide, and the more simple the language must be. Reports may also have a persuasive element, such as recommending one of three ways to deal with storm-water pollution.
- *Specifications.* Specifications are normally written for those who will be performing tasks. They are usually experts in those tasks. Clarity and

precision are the most important language considerations. The objective of specifications is most often to document the project requirements.

- *Manuals.* Usually written to instruct, manuals provide step-by-step methods to complete tasks. Clarity and completeness is important, and the audience's existing knowledge on the topic needs to be understood.
- *Technical articles.* The technical article is most often written for other experts and printed in technical journals. The primary objective is to increase knowledge.
- *Mass print media.* The mass print media (newspapers and magazines) are increasingly looking for experts to write material for publication. The audience obviously is on the other extreme from the expert. The objective is almost always to increase knowledge.

Business and Managerial Messages

Increased use of persuasion as an objective distinguishes business and managerial written messages from technical messages. The emphasis is less on technical topics and more on human interaction.

- *Proposals.* Proposals persuade an audience to select an option. That option could be to hire your firm to perform consulting services or for your board of directors to hire more staff. How you present your persuasive message depends on the audience needs and expectations.
- *Marketing.* Marketing involves increasing knowledge about your organization and persuading the receiver to use your services. Some common examples of printed marketing messages are brochures, letters, newsletters, or press releases.
- *Letters, memos, faxes, E-mail, and other electronic print delivery.* The business world runs on these forms of written communication. The objectives can be any of our four, and the audiences vary as widely.

SOURCES OF NOISE

Noise that prevents receivers from understanding written messages takes many forms. The main places to look for noise include selection of knowledge, message structure, language usage, and message design. The following list presents common noise sources; each will be discussed in more detail in the following chapters.

- *Poor logic.* When we run across poor logic we usually scratch our heads and say, "But that doesn't make sense."

- *Omission.* Omission refers to knowledge left out of the message and needed for complete understanding.
- *Redundancy.* The opposite of omission, redundancy refers to unnecessary repetition of knowledge. Repetition, if done correctly, is an excellent way to increase knowledge. But redundancy is merely noise.
- *Poor paragraphing.* Paragraphs were created for a reason—to help readers comprehend written text. But if the writer ignores the guidelines for paragraphing, he may as well run words together without punctuation.
- *Unclear wording or jargon.* We can choose from the thousands of words to get our message across. Some words are better than others as a rule, some are better than others in specific cases, depending on our audience.
- *Unnecessary words or phrases.* We tend to fill up our sentences with words or phrases that do not help with understanding.
- *Incorrect grammar, improper punctuation, and misspellings.* These types of noise can quickly reduce your credibility.
- *Poor page design and typography.* Visual noise on the printed page can be caused by clutter, wrong typeface choice, and other details.

The rest of the chapters in this part of the book explain how to reduce the noise. One of the main themes to be introduced is that written language should be clear and concise. Another theme is that written messages must be structured logically and paragraphs used correctly. Sentences should be simple and direct, and words correctly chosen. Page design should be uncluttered and balanced.

WRITER'S BLOCK: THE MYTH

"I just can't write now. Must be writer's block." We've all heard about the affliction called writer's block. But there isn't a common definition. Each writer has her or his definition based on individual experience. One writer defines it as the dread or fear or inability to sit down and write, even if the writer knows what he wants to say. To another writer it's the feeling of being all used up, that there's nothing left to write about. Another calls it "writer's reluctance," which may be simple procrastination.

Whatever the cause, writer's block may not really be a block. It's simply that writing, as already said, is difficult. No one enjoys difficult tasks, especially when we haven't been given a clear procedure to follow. As an engineer, you can solve complex problems in your sleep, literally. You probably haven't written anything in your sleep, although you might have had nightmares about it. I know I have.

That's why I introduced the concept of approaching communication, and especially writing, as a problem solving exercise. It takes advantage of your logic and precise analytic mind. Of course, you will need to practice, just as you practiced solving problems in engineering courses. Practice, practice, practice.

Pretty soon you'll be able to write in your sleep, or at least not have nightmares about writing.

SUMMARY

This chapter started by explaining why writing is so difficult. If we know why writing is difficult then perhaps we can simplify the process. Of course, nobody will say that good writing is easy. But then bad writing isn't easy either. This chapter also introduced the types of common written messages and how their topics, audience considerations, and objectives vary. Several types of noise found in written messages were described.

The next chapters try to make good writing easier and reduce that stress.

Chapter 7

STRUCTURAL DESIGN OF WRITTEN COMMUNICATION

> Form follows function.

Figure 8.
Form Follows Function #1

In this chapter, the overall structural design of written messages—as opposed to the component parts, such as paragraphs, sentences, words, punctuation—is introduced. The term "structural design" was intentionally chosen to make an analogy to the structural design of buildings.

Figure 9.
Form Follows Function #2

The structural design of written communications also refers to message organization; that is, the flow of knowledge. To carry the analogy further, this chapter presents a way to organize messages the same way an architect plans the flow of people in buildings. And, of course, the TAO communication principles will be used to structure written communications.

STRUCTURE TEMPLATES

All structures are designed and built for a purpose. That purpose dictates the size, layout, structural design, and even the building's finish. That's why a state capitol (Figure 8) has a gilded dome, and why a burrito wagon (Figure 9) is topped with a sombrero. That's why a parking garage (Figure 10) is different from a single-family home (Figure 11).

**Figure 10.
Form Follows Function #3**

A building's purpose provides designers with a *template*—a generic pattern—to start their design. Templates give buildings a preliminary shape, size, layout, and rough costs.

When people enter a building, they have that building's template in mind. These templates are expectations derived from experience. For example, if they're entering a high-rise office building (Figure 12), they expect to find a lobby with elevators and a building directory, maybe a security guard. If they walk into a lobby of an apartment building (Figure 13), they are probably expecting to see a directory of the residents and a phone or intercom system.

What if they walked into the lobby of an office building and found a maitre d' passing out menus? Or if they walked up to the burrito wagon and found a state legislature in session? They would be very confused because their expectations would be violated.

**Figure 11.
Form Follows Function #4**

That's why written-message templates are as important as building templates. We don't want to have our audience start out confused. Most audiences have an idea of how a report, technical manual, memo, or business letter should be structured. Help the audience with a clear message structure that facilitates understanding and doesn't violate their expectations.

The previous chapter presented the main categories of written messages. These categories can be thought of as templates in that they provide the audience an indication of the scope and purpose of the message. Comparing some of these categories to buildings might be an interesting exercise:

Specifications	=	Libraries
Technical reports	=	Office buildings
Manuals	=	Warehouses
Corporate annual reports	=	Art museums
Memos	=	Burrito wagons

Then again, it might not be.

Figure 12.
Form Follows Function #5

Figure 13.
Form Follows Function #6

TOPIC KNOWLEDGE ORGANIZATION

The concept of a message template is a bit abstract, of course, and to make use of message templates we need to add substance. A building designer, for example, might have to choose the number, size, and location of offices and conference rooms. For written messages, senders need to determine which portion of their knowledge to use and how to organize it.

To select the appropriate knowledge to include in the message, the sender needs only to refer to their sorted knowledge structures. The audience and objective determine the appropriate level of detail.

The next step is to organize the knowledge. For example, in some reports an executive summary should come first, in other reports an introduction should come first. In a proposal should you discuss your company's experience first or get straight to the point? When do you discuss the methods of the study? Do you start from the broad to the narrow or from the narrow to the broad? The answers, again, depend on your audience and objective, so let's look at their application in detail.

Audience and Objective Considerations

Assuming you've got a good handle on your audience and their characteristics you can organize message flow by answering the following questions:

What does the audience know about the topic?

What knowledge do they need to understand the message?

The first question helps establish what knowledge comes first. If your report is to a store owners' group about the effects of a paving program on access to their property, then they wouldn't need to know about asphalt concrete strength and subbase construction. They want to know how long their customers will be without normal access to the shops.

The same report on the street-paving program would start out different if it was to be written for a group of developers who will be footing part of the bill. Then the asphalt concrete strength and subbase construction would be more important because it affects the costs of the project.

The Bubble Technique for Organizing

When architects or space planners design the interior of a building, they often use a bubble diagram. Figure 14 is an example.

Figure 14. Office Building Bubble Diagram

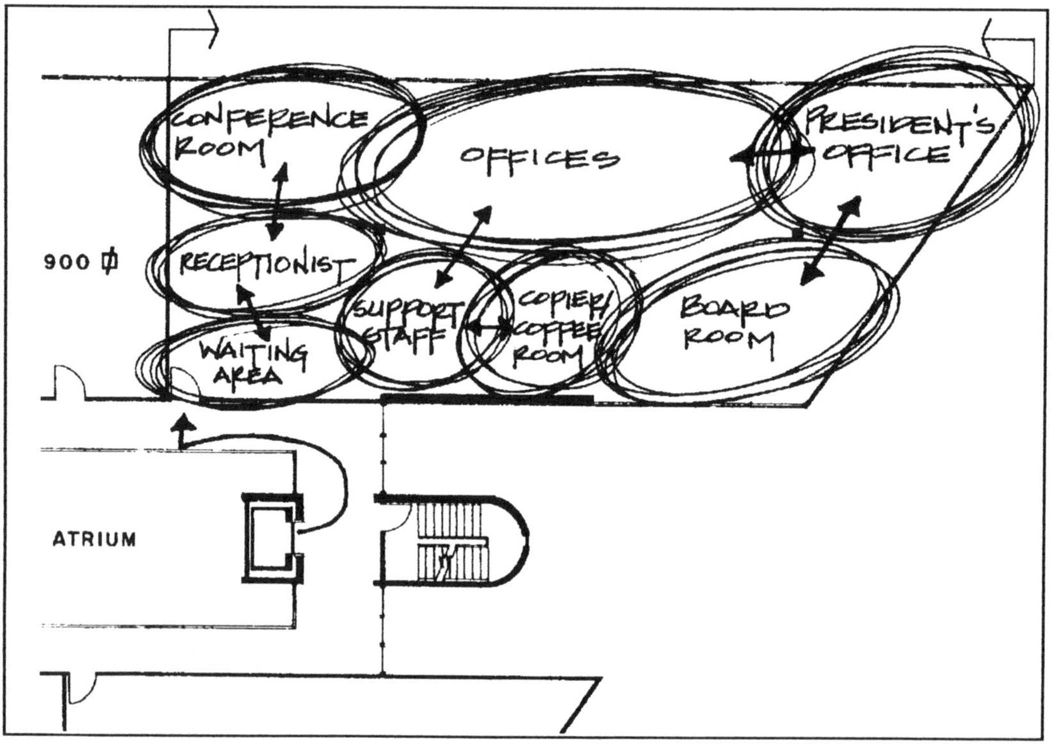

The same type of flow diagram can be used to organize a report. Figure 15 is an example based on a report of earthquake damage to a water utility.

Figure 15. Bubble Diagram for a Report

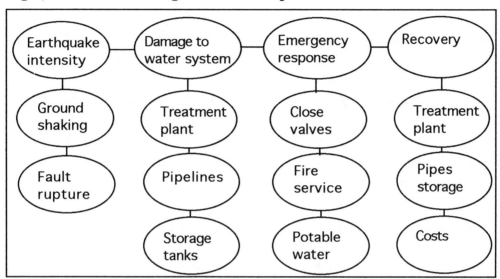

The bubbles give a general placement of knowledge, as well as represent different levels of knowledge. The bubbles can also represent sections of a longer message, each with its own heading.

Using bubbles is also a good way to brainstorm. You can start with the bubbles as they come to your mind, then draw lines that connect them. The method is good if you're stuck as to what should be next in your message.

MESSAGE LENGTH

Remember in school when you were assigned to write a composition? Wasn't the first question asked of the teacher: How long does it have to be? If the assigned length was five pages, then you probably wouldn't want to write on the Rise and Fall of the Soviet Union. You'd probably have to leave out a couple of events of historical value. Of course, you wouldn't want to try to fit an essay on why your cat's name is Scooter into ten pages. You'd have a lot of padding to come up with.

But in reality we often are told how long our messages are to be, for example, the proposal of twenty pages, the article of 5,000 words, the manual of 100 pages. The trick is to not hurt your message by forcing it unnaturally into a required length. Applying the correct level of detail will usually keep a message in the correct length.

When you control the length of your message, then the following rule applies: Written messages should be complete and as short as possible.

OUTLINE OR JUMP IN

With a general organization established for a message, the next step is to begin the first draft. There are two general approaches: jump right in, or outline in detail.

Outlining uses basically the same organizing techniques used for the overall document. Use the bubble technique for each section of the message. You can progress to the paragraph level with this technique.

The jump-right-in technique involves writing whatever comes to mind for the section. Of course, that means going back and cleaning it up later. But the method can free your mind from constraints, allowing the free flow of ideas that often might not have otherwise surfaced. Some writers do this kind of writing as fast as possible, not bothering to clean up typos or worry about punctuation. Other writers can't stand to do this method, claiming it merely produces a lot of junk. Some writers combine the methods.

Which approach you use depends on your own style. Do whatever works to get the first draft down on paper (or on that computer screen). The following chapters will give specific guidelines on writing the first draft and polishing it into the final draft.

SUMMARY

The main theme of this chapter is that logical flow of information depends on message templates which meet your audience's expectations and your communication objectives. Bubble diagrams were suggested as a technique for organizing information. Tips were given on the lengths of written messages and writing the first draft. The following chapter discusses the next level of complexity in written messages: the paragraph.

Chapter 8

EFFECTIVE PARAGRAPHS

> Pity the poor paragraph—mistreated, misused, and misunderstood.

Ask several people, "What's a paragraph?" and quite often the answer will be: "It's where you put in a TAB."

Well, yes, you ask, but why a TAB there, at that particular place? "Well, I thought the paragraph was getting a little long," or, "I ran out of steam and thought starting a new paragraph would help," or, "I learned that the average paragraph has five sentences." Another popular answer is: "It's where a single thought starts, isn't it? Or is that a sentence?"

Although each answer has a bit of truth, they miss the point of paragraphs. In this chapter the reasons for the existence of paragraphs are presented, as well as guidelines for paragraph construction.

PURPOSE OF PARAGRAPHS

To begin with, let's continue with the analogy to buildings. As the structure of written messages was compared to buildings, a good paragraph can be compared to a single room in a building. For instance, consider the floor plan of a single-family home shown in Figure 16.

Each of the rooms was designed for a main purpose. The kitchen is where we cook, the living room is where we socialize, and so on. As with overall building plans, where form follows function, the size and shape of rooms depends on their purpose. For example, a dining room must accommodate a table with four to six or more chairs and a hutch or two. It needs to be close to the kitchen.

Paragraphs should be treated with the same deliberation. Each paragraph has a single main purpose, a single main idea, a view. And a paragraph is filled up with only the furniture (sentences) necessary to fulfill its function.

Figure 16. Rooms Represent Paragraphs

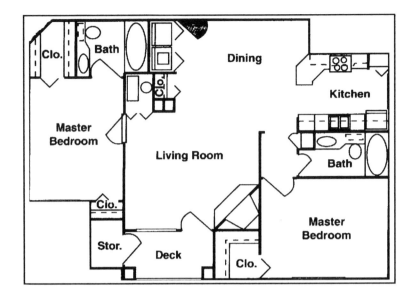

Why do paragraphs start with a tab or line break? The same reason we have walls or dividers in a house—to set off the rooms from each other, so their unique purposes can be separated. Paragraph breaks signal to the reader that a new idea is about to begin. And this will help readers understand the message because they can more easily remember the idea. Paragraph breaks also give readers a place to rest or reflect.

Sounds easy enough, right? It can be, but unfortunately, it's not often done well. But with the guidelines presented in this chapter the task can become easier. The guidelines include writing paragraphs with a single idea or node, making paragraphs the ideal length, and using the classic paragraph construction technique.

SINGLE IDEA AS NODE

When does a paragraph have a single idea? For that matter, what's an idea? A difficult concept to define, but for our purposes let's consider a single idea as a node or point in a sorted knowledge structure, at the most detailed level. The single idea is something the reader can easily grasp with one hand (or one group of brain cells). A single idea can be expressed in one phrase.

Table 2 illustrates the concept of a single idea. The topic is hazardous materials releases that can contaminate drinking water systems.

Table 2. Nodes and Paragraphs

Node phrase	Paragraph
Hazardous materials: types used by water systems	Any material that can harm humans or contaminate air or water should be considered hazardous. Hazardous materials used in water treatment include chlorine, fluorosilicic acid, ferric acid, and small amounts of sulfuric acid. Other materials are also used by utilities not related directly to treatment including cleaning solutions, gasoline, antifreeze, and oils. The materials become a problem when spilled or accidentally released.
Hazardous materials spills by others	Spills or releases of hazardous materials by others can also contaminate drinking water systems. The materials can be liquid, solid, or gaseous. Spills commonly originate from pipelines, manufacturing plants, or transportation vehicles. Spills can occur at any time of day or night.

As you can see, the node phrase is the equivalent of one bit of information. The node phrase can also be thought of as a level in an outline. The paragraph expands on the node in as much detail as is necessary to help the audience understand the concept.

LENGTH

Paragraphs need to be as long as they need to be. Great, you say. So, what does that mean? How long is an idea? Paragraph length depends on the complexity of the idea, and how it fits in with the other ideas in adjacent paragraphs. An idea is as long as an idea needs to be, whether it's one sentence or twenty.

But I did promise you some guidelines. Okay, a rule of thumb is that a paragraph is four to seven sentences long. Four to seven … that sounds familiar. Right, the short-term memory holds up to four to seven chunks of information.

Of course, paragraphs can be shorter or longer than four to seven sentences. Shorter, if the single idea is less complex or needs no elaboration, longer only when necessary and when written so the reader doesn't lose the idea that you're trying to get across. If your paragraph is too long, check to see if two or more ideas are lurking. Then give each idea its own paragraph. For example, the following paragraph can be separated into two ideas to improve the logical flow.

> Critical water-system components are those vulnerable to failure because of a disaster hazard. Identifying them is an important step in making a water system less vulnerable to disasters. The failure of a system component will reduce the ability of a utility to meet minimum public health and safety goals. The best way to approach identifying critical components is to assume a disaster scenario. Different types of disasters will affect components differently. Focus on the components that are interrelated with other components that would make the entire system inoperative: these are the most vulnerable components. Assume the component is out of operation and then see how this affects the rest of the system. You can use a computer model to simulate the loss. Repeat the process with other disaster scenarios. The goal is to meet priority demand, which is the minimum needed to maintain public health and safety.

Did you see two main ideas in the paragraph? How about these:
- The nature of critical components and public safety.
- The process of identifying critical components.

The paragraph could be rewritten into two paragraphs as follows:

> Critical water-system components are those vulnerable to failure because of disaster hazards. The goal of a water utility is to meet priority demand, which is the minimum needed to maintain public health and safety. The failure of a system component will reduce the ability of a utility to meet the goals. Identifying critical components is an important step in making a water system less vulnerable to disasters.

> The best way to approach identifying critical components is to assume a disaster scenario. Different types of disasters will affect components differently. Focus on the components that are interrelated with other components that would make the entire system inoperative: these are the most critical components. Assume the component is out of operation and then see how this affects the rest of the system. You can use a computer model to simulate the loss. Repeat the process with other disaster scenarios.

Writing instructors often tell their students to vary the length of their paragraphs. If you're writing good paragraphs, using the single idea technique, then your paragraphs will naturally vary in length. Each idea is naturally more or less complex than any other idea.

CLASSIC PARAGRAPH CONSTRUCTION

The classic paragraph consists of the focus statement, the support statements, and the transition. Each is described in the following sections and is illustrated with examples.

Focus Statement

The focus statement contains the central idea or node of the paragraph. Except in rare circumstances (where support statements such as examples are given first) the focus statement is at the beginning of the paragraph. In the example, the focus statements are in bold.

> **Critical water-system components are those vulnerable to failure because of disaster hazards.** The goal of a water...
>
> **The best way to approach identifying critical components is to assume a disaster scenario.** Different types ...

Support Statements

Support statements clarify or elaborate on the focus statement. They can be examples that illustrate the idea, the steps in a process, or simply more detail about the focus statement. The sentences in bold are support statements.

> Critical ... The goal of a water utility is to meet priority demand, which is the minimum needed to maintain public health and safety. The failure of a system component will reduce the ability of a utility to meet the goals. Identifying ...
>
> The best ... Different types of disasters will affect components differently. Focus on the components that are interrelated with other components that would make the entire system inoperative: these are the most critical components. Assume the component is out of operation and then see how this affects the rest of the system. You can use a computer model to simulate the loss. Repeat the process with other disaster scenarios.

Transition Statement

Transitions help paragraphs flow together, rather than jump from one idea to the next. The sentence in bold in the example smoothes the way for the next paragraph.

> Critical water system ... meet the goals. **Identifying critical components is an important step in making a water system less vulnerable to disasters.**
>
> The best way to approach identifying critical components is to assume a disaster scenario. Different ...

SUMMARY

Paragraphs are often overlooked in the pursuit of good writing. Yet they are one of the fundamental building blocks of logical flow of knowledge. Paragraphs can be easily constructed when each is limited to a single idea. The classic paragraph construction—consisting of the focus statement, support statements, and a transition statement—is an excellent way to help an audience understand written messages.

Good paragraphs, like good rooms, have a view.

Chapter 9

GOOD SENTENCES

So far, we've looked at the overall organization of written messages and paragraphs. Now it's time to get down to the nitty-gritty of sentences. First, this chapter deals with that horror word—grammar. You'll be shown a gentle and simple way of looking at grammar that takes advantage of engineers' superior math ability. Any grammarphobia should be cured or at least tempered. Then, the characteristics of a good sentence will be presented, along with easy-to-remember rules.

OVERCOMING GRAMMARPHOBIA

Let's start with a test. You have a choice of two tasks:

Task #1: Simplify this equation and solve for *x*:

$$9x^3 - 6x^2 + 3x = 2$$

Task #2: Parse this sentence:

It should be understood from the beginning that the purpose of the chlorine-residual analyzer discussed here is to control the chlorine dose.

Most engineers will probably want to tackle Task #1. They instantly understand the terms *simplify* and *solve for*. They recognize each part of the equations: 9, 6, 3, and 2 are constants; *x* is the unknown; and the equals sign. At a glance, they can see that the equation can be solved.

What about the second task? "Parse," of course, means "to resolve a sentence into component parts of speech and describe them grammatically." Grammar is nothing more than a convention or set of rules, like agreed-on math symbols, or calling apples apples, and oranges oranges. Without grammar, we wouldn't have a very sophisticated language.

This discussion of grammar won't go into every rule, every verb tense or mood; whole books are written on the subject. Grammar really is a fascinating story, but this chapter concentrates on those areas where we most often go wrong.

THE SENTENCE EQUATION

Let's start at the beginning. A sentence is a complete thought; in mathematical terms, a sentence can be thought of as a balanced equation. What constitutes a balanced equation in a grammar sense? Generally, it means having an *actor* and an *action*.

Simply put, the actor does the action. In grammar terminology, an actor is the *subject* of the sentence. Subjects are nouns or pronouns. And actions are *verbs*.

>The engineer spoke.
>She wrote.
>The homeowner read.

$$\text{Actor} + \text{Action} = \text{Sentence}$$
$$\text{-or-}$$
$$S + V = T$$

Where:
$$S = \text{Subject}$$
$$V = \text{Verb}$$
$$T = \text{Thought (complete)}$$

Now, more on verbs. The two basic kinds are transitive and intransitive. Transitive verbs take an object; intransitive verbs do not. An object receives the action from the subject; it is what is acted upon by the actor.

>The column supports *the roof*.
>She wrote *the report*.

Substituting the two verb forms, our sentence equation becomes:

$$S + V_i = T$$
$$S + (V_t + O) = T$$

Where:
$$S = \text{Subject}$$
$$V_i = \text{Intransitive Verb}$$
$$V_t = \text{Transitive Verb}$$
$$O = \text{Object}$$

SENTENCE SIMPLIFICATION

Sentence simplification means reducing a sentence to its $S + V$ form. We want to simplify sentences because the basic sentence structure, $S + V$, is the overall best sentence structure, for many reasons.

We also simplify sentences for the same reasons we simplify mathematical equations—to make them easier to solve and to see if they balance. The goal of sentence simplification is to reduce a sentence to its essence; that is, to find its subject and verb. For example, find the subject and verb in the following sentence from *Engineering as a Social Enterprise* (National Academy of Engineering, 1990):

> In a series of four articles in *Technology and Culture*, Walter Vincenti, an aeronautical engineer and historian, also provides a thoughtful and informative reading of the technology-science relationship.

The subject is *Walter Vincenti*, and the verb is *provides*. Because *provides* is a transitive verb in this case, it needs an object, which is *a reading*.

$$
\underset{S}{\text{Walter Vincenti}} \quad \underset{+\ V_t}{\text{provides}} \quad \underset{+\ O}{\text{a reading}} \quad = \quad T
$$

We have a balanced sentence, a complete thought. If any of the components were missing, we wouldn't have a complete thought. We'd have a *sentence fragment*. In mathematics, we'd have an unbalanced equation. One exception: a sentence can exist without a subject or verb, as long as it's understood. For example: "How did the meeting go?" "Fine." Obviously we understand it was the *meeting* (subject) that *went* (verb) fine.

The words other than the subject or verb or object provide additional meaning to the basic sentence. They are called *modifiers*, and are adjectives, adverbs, clauses, and phrases. For example, Walter Vincenti is described as an aeronautical engineer and historian, and the reading is described as thoughtful and informative.

Modifiers cause most of the problems in sentences because they tend to get tangled up with what they are modifying. To help untangle the mess the best way is to simplify the sentence into $S + V + O$.

Now let's use sentence simplification to solve a common sentence problem: agreement.

AGREEMENT

Agreement means that the verb form must agree with the subject, or the modifiers must agree with the words they modify. For example, *I calculate the co-efficients*, as opposed to *I calculates the coefficients*. Or this more complex example:

Wrong	Right
Failing to shut the correct valve, the effluent discharged into the storm drain.	When the operator failed to shut the correct valve, the effluent discharged into the storm drain.

The more words we have in a sentence the more chances we have to mess up agreement. That's why we simplify. By temporarily stripping out all the modifiers, we find that *effluent* is the subject and it could not have been responsible for shutting the valve; we must give credit to the operator.

Pronouns particularly cause agreement trouble. Pronouns are used as subjects, objects, possessives, or reflexives. The following box lists the subject, object, and possessive cases.

Subject	Object	Possessive
I	me	my, mine
you	you	your, yours
he	him	his
she	her	hers
they	them	their, theirs
we	us	our, ours
who	whom	whose
it	it	its

Be sure to use the correct pronoun case. Simplify the sentence if it isn't immediately clear which form is correct as shown in these examples:

Wrong	Right
Bill and me had a hand in the water tower design.	... *I* had a hand ...

Wrong	Right
The cause of the water tower collapse left him and I baffled.	The cause ... left ... *me* baffled.
I was surprised at him resigning.	... *his* resigning [possessive case]
The new engineer, who I met in school, will redesign the tower.	... *whom* I met ... [I is the subject of the clause, not who. We could say "... who met me in school ..."]
The tower failed because it's foundation was inadequate.	... *its* foundation ... [possessive case. It's, a contraction, means it is and only it is]

GRAMMAR CHECKERS

Before getting into good sentence construction, a word on computer grammar checkers should be said. The word is *someday*. Someday they will be valuable. Right now they do little, other than look for sentences that start with *and*. They also spend a lot of time looking for passive sentences (discussed later in this chapter), which is good, but that's often the least of the sentence's problems. For example, the grammar checkers I've used won't flag this sentence as wrong: *Yesterday, I run to the store.*

Grammar checkers do calculate a readability index, which rates writing with an approximate grade level. The indexes are usually calculated from a formula based on sentence and word length. The longer the sentences and words, the more difficult the reading. The index can be a start at finding out if you're writing to your audience. Most newspapers are written at sixth to eighth grade level, and messages for the general public should be in that range. Technical articles are usually written at college sophomore level. Any writing over that level probably could be written more concisely.

GOOD SENTENCE PRINCIPLES

The two principles of good sentences are simply that a good sentence is clear, and a good sentence is concise.

A clear and concise sentence is almost invisible; the reader glides over it effortlessly. The sentence meaning leaps to mind; the reader doesn't have to struggle to find it. An unclear sentence is noisy. The following tips on sentence length, active vs. passive sentences, and trusting your ear will help you write clear and concise sentences.

Length

Sentences that are long (25 words is an approximate trigger point) should be inspected. Check for needless words and eliminate them. The sentence may have two or more sentences tangled together; sort them out and give them unique identities. Look at the following examples to see how to sort out tangled sentences.

Noisy	Clear and concise
The efficiency of treatment plant operations is best measured by the relationships between costs incurred and amounts of work accomplished usually measured in terms of physical units, the cost per unit being determined by dividing total costs applicable to a number of units of work performed by the number of units.	Operational efficiency of treatment plants is best measured by comparing costs incurred and work accomplished. Work is usually measured in physical units, [such as ...]. Divide total applicable costs by the number of units to obtain the cost per unit work.
The agency, under certain circumstances, may find it desirable to approve a temporary connection to the potable water system in the event of a situation where all or a portion of the reclaimed water is not in service.	The agency may approve a temporary connection to the potable water system if reclaimed water is not available.

Active vs. Passive

Active sentences are better than passive sentences. In an active sentence, we use our $S + V$ sentence equation; in passive sentences, the subject may be buried and left for dead.

Passive	Active
Work that meets the specifications completed on time by the contractor shall be paid for in full by the owner.	The owner shall pay the contractor in full for work that is on time and meets the specifications.

To make a passive sentence active, find the subject and verb and restore them to their rightful positions. That is: $S + V + O$. The passive sentence in the example was written as $O + V + S$. When you use active sentences instead of passive, sentences will naturally become clear and concise.

Your Ear

Trust your ear. Read your sentences out loud, if that helps. If a sentence sounds confusing, it probably is. Take a close look at it. Is it confusing because it's noisy, or because you're confused on the point you're trying to make? Explain it out loud, as if you were trying to explain your point to a friend.

Also, trust your ear when reading several sentences together. Are they all the same length? That will probably sound too monotonous. Vary the length without violating the sentence principles. As with paragraphs, if you use the correct principles, your sentences will naturally vary.

SUMMARY

This chapter presented a mathematical approach to grammar and sentence structure. This approach allows a writer to simplify sentences to solve many sentence construction problems, such as agreement, length, and passive sentences. The most important tip to remember from this chapter is that a good sentence is clear and concise.

Chapter 10

WORDS AND PUNCTUATION

So far in our pursuit of good writing, we've looked at the structure of written messages, paragraph construction, and good sentences. What's next is to discuss the next level: words and phrases, and punctuation. The quote that follows is from *The Elements of Style*, a small book that contains many gems of good writing advice.

Omit needless words!

William Strunk, Jr.

WORDS AND PHRASES

Choices—that's what this section is all about. It gives important guidelines to help us choose the best word. The overriding guideline, of course, is to use communication principles. Which word will best be understood by our audience? Which word or phrase best meets the objective of our communication? By choosing the correct words, we will also be reducing noise.

Be Careful with Jargon

Jargon is special language understood only by those in the field. Jargon can be technical terms (95% Proctor, C-value), acronyms and initialisms (HEC-2, SWMM), and other cryptic references (camera the sewer). Jargon is fine to use when you're sure of your audience's familiarity; don't use it when the audience isn't familiar with it unless you define the word or phrase.

Use Correct Words

When a word is misused it can confuse the reader. To avoid misuse, the careful writer will make sure each word is being used correctly. Most good dictionaries include correct usage rules with the definitions of commonly misused words.

When in doubt, look up the word in the dictionary. The following list includes commonly misused words and the correct usage. Most reference books on writing have several other such words.

That and *which*. *That* is used with a defining (restrictive) phrase; in other words, the phrase is necessary to define the exact thing you're talking about. (Only the test results *that* showed a failure need to be checked.) *Which* is used with a descriptive (nonrestrictive) phrase. A *which* phrase is normally set off with commas. (The test results, *which* all showed a failure, need to be checked.)

Continuous and *continual*. *Continuous* means never stopping. (The pump ran *continuously* through the night.) *Continual* means to recur regularly or frequently. (The pump has broken down *continually* since we installed it.)

Affect and *effect*. *Affect* is a verb meaning to influence. (How will the additional pavement *affect* the runoff?) *Effect* is used most commonly as a noun meaning the result or outcome. (The *effect* of more pavement will be an increase in runoff.) Refer to the next section ("Be specific and strong") for more discussion on affect and effect.

Alternate and *alternative*. *Alternate* means to switch back and forth. (We *alternate* the two pumps to keep from burning them out.) *Alternative* means a choice. (The *alternative* to using both pumps is to keep one in storage.)

Data and *datum*. When data refers to facts or results, it is plural. (The *data* show a clear trend.) When data means information, it is singular. (Good *data* is important when making a decision.) Datum, meaning a single fact, is rarely used anymore.

Be Specific and Strong

Specific and strong words are better than abstract and weak words. Specific and strong words are more easily remembered, and they make writing more interesting. Writing with strong and specific words takes more effort *but is very important to good writing*. Here are some examples:

Abstract and weak	Specific and strong
Ground shaking during earthquakes can affect foundations.	Ground shaking during earthquakes cracks and weakens foundations.
The effect of your decision is a major change in our department.	Your decision will reduce our staff 20% and force us to hire contract labor.

Abstract and weak	Specific and strong
The concern with regard to service connections on a dual water system is the potential for cross connections between the potable and nonpotable systems.	Cross connections between potable and nonpotable water systems could contaminate service connections.
The wetland area should be left in an undisturbed state.	Do not enter the wetlands.
The bridge has unique characteristics.	The bridge is unique because it uses less reinforcing steel and longer spans.

Use Positive Words

Positive words are better than negative words because people can more easily figure out what you're saying, or what you want them to do. For example, I said, "Use positive words," rather than, "Do not use negative words." Also watch the tone of your words; be sensitive to nuance. "I believe you failed to understand what I proposed" puts the reader immediately on the defensive. Instead, say "Perhaps I could have explained my proposal better."

Rewrite Clichés, Stilted Phrases, or Overused Phrases

Readers want modern, fresh, and original writing. Don't write like Shakespeare or an attorney, or especially Shakespeare's attorney. Here are some examples:

Shakespeare's attorney	Modern
at such time	when
resulting from an action by the user	caused
agreed-upon resolutions of issues	agreements
the manner in which	how
herein	in
in the event that	if
heretofore	previous

Clichés	Fresh
state of the art	latest
in a nutshell	concise
ballpark figure	estimate
par for the course	expected

Two phrases that can often be eliminated are "It is" and "There is." The phrases often hide the subject. For example, "It is a complex project." Why not simply say: "The project is complex"? When we do, we return the subject of the sentence ("project") to the beginning of the sentence where it belongs. Other examples are:

"There are two equations you can use to solve the problem." Rewrite as: "You can use two equations to solve the problem."

"It is particularly important that the solutions be homogenous." Instead: "The solutions must be homogenous."

Use Contractions and Pronouns

Use contractions and pronouns, except in the most formal writing (even that is changing). Contractions and pronouns sound less formal, and more conversational and modern. Most readers sound out the words in their minds as they read and will mentally change "we will" to "we'll," and "do not" to "don't."

Watch Out for Repetitious Phrases

The classic example of a repetitious phrase for journalists is "dead body." ("The murder victim's dead body was found.") If a body is found, the person has to be dead. A few other examples are:

- completely destroyed (destroy means to ruin completely)
- different varieties (a variety implies differences)
- final outcome (outcome means the final result)
- overall plan (plan is perfectly fine by itself)
- prior preparation (one prepares beforehand)
- whether or not (whether implies the choice of two)

Use Parallel Phrasing

Use consistent verb tense or phrase construction within a sentence or paragraph. Otherwise, the writing is noisy. For example:

Noisy	Parallel
The steps to take a water sample include using a clean jar, turn on the tap slowly, filling the jar to the line, then you turn off the tap slowly, and be sure to seal the jar with the lid.	The steps to take a water sample are: use a clean jar, turn on the tap slowly, fill the jar to the line, turn off the tap slowly, and seal the jar with the lid.

Can you see the difference? In the noisy sentence, the verbs were: using, turn on, filling, turn off, and be sure. The parallel sentence used only the imperative (command) form: use, turn on, fill, turn off, and seal.

Use Nonsexist and Unbiased Words or Phrases

The most common problem is the use of the pronoun "he" when referring to a generic person who could be male or female. The usual alternatives are "he or she" or "they" (be sure to check agreement). However, as you may have noticed in this book, other ways can be used. I alternate "he" and "she" because of the heavy use of pronouns. "He or she" or "they" got a little tedious. If you use this method, "she" should be used the first time a pronoun is used so your audience isn't initially put off. Other methods are used, but they tend to be awkward: s/he, (s)he, always writing in the plural (using "they"). Genderless nouns work well ("homeowners" or "engineers" or "writers"), although they too can become tedious.

Other nonsexist terms should be used such as "chair" for "chairman," and "staff hours" for "man hours." Also, do not perpetuate stereotypes or trample on other cultures' values.

Spell and Capitalize Correctly

Nothing lowers a communicator's image as much as misspellings. Computer spell checkers help a little more than grammar checkers do with grammar, but are still imperfect. If you've used them, you know that the reasons are obvious: they can only tell if a word is on their list. "Red" is spelled correctly only if you meant the color, not if you meant to spell "read." Use the checkers if you want, but don't rely on them to catch all your mistakes.

The only capitalization rule *never* to follow is: When in doubt, capitalize. Most capitalization is obvious, but two rules are frequently violated.

- Capitalize peoples' titles only when they precede the person's name (President Bill Clinton; or, Bill Clinton, president of the United States).
- Capitalize trade names (Xerox, Sheetrock). When in doubt, look it up.

PUNCTUATION MADE SIMPLE

Simple? What's so simple about punctuation? The mystery of the correct use of the comma has befuddled more than mere mortals. What's the purpose of punctuation? More than one writing instructor puts it this way: Punctuation is visual representation of oral inflection.

Listen to the way you speak. You pause in various lengths, longest for the break between paragraphs, shortest between hyphenated words. Punctuation helps the reader understand the meaning of the words you put together as if you were speaking them. Traffic signs and pavement markings function the same way; they help drivers negotiate a roadway.

Read the following sentences to see how the length of the pause changes:

The diagram needs a legend of the symbols.

The diagram needs a legend, or more standard symbols.

The diagram needs a legend. I can't understand the symbols.

The diagram needs a legend. I can't understand—although it's my fault—the symbols.

Let's look at specific punctuation marks and the most common applications.

- *Commas.* Separate items in lists (The items are indicators, test tubes, and flasks...), and set off descriptive phrases (...indicators, which are red, green or blue, and...) and adjacent adjectives or adverbs (...the test tubes are glass, small, and marked). As with the when-in-doubt-capital-ize rule, do not put in a comma when in doubt. Listen to the sentence.
- *Semicolons.* Join two complete sentences which are better off together than apart (The items are packed in the box; don't drop it.) Semicolons also help out with lists having items embedded with commas (...blue, red, and green indicators; test tubes; and flasks.)
- *Colons.* Introduce a list or a definitive statement. (The items are: ...)
- *Parentheses.* Set off a phrase as an aside, which is almost like a foot-note. [The street design parameters (as found in the manual's appendix) are based on empirical data.]
- *Quotation marks.* Use for quotations or words introduced as terms. (The name "dead-end" will no longer be used on street signs.)
- *Dashes.* Also called an "m" dash, because it takes as much space as the letter m. Similar to parentheses when used with an aside.
- *Hyphens.* Join words together to avoid confusion as to which word is modifying which word. For example: Take two quart samples. Does

this mean two one-quart samples? Or does it mean to take one two-quart sample?

- *Bullets vs. numbers.* Use bullets for lists, numbers for steps that must be completed in order.
- *Slashes.* Most style references recommend against using a slash to connect words such as and/or. Write precisely what you mean. (The items may include indicators and/or flasks. The items may include indicators, flasks, or both.)

SUMMARY

In this chapter we looked at the building blocks of sentences: words, phrases, and punctuation. We have to make choices continually as we write. A few easy-to-remember guidelines were presented and illustrated with examples. Keep a few good reference books at hand; a list can be found in the bibliography.

Make good choices and your writing will sparkle.

Chapter 11

EDITING

Editing is a process that improves written documents. Engineering plans aren't let out the door without a quality check. Written documents shouldn't be either; they say as much about an organization as do engineering plans. Unfortunately, many documents are spell-checked and that's about it.

You've probably asked a colleague, "Could you look over this letter [or report or memo] for me?"

"Sure," he says. He sharpens his red pencil, finds a couple of misspelled words, notes a couple of awkward sentences, and hands back the document.

"Looks good," he says.

"Thanks. You're a gentleman and a scholar."

If you've read the first eleven chapters of this book, you'd probably guess that editing involves much more. This chapter presents editing guidelines for quality-checking documents.

EDITING CATEGORIES

Before discussing specific editing skills, I'd like to point out the differences in editing your own work, having others edit your work, and editing others' work.

Self-Editing

Editing your own work doesn't replace having others edit it, but you'll want to do it anyway. It doesn't replace having someone else edit it because often it's difficult to see your own unclear ideas. You're too close to the work, and you understand the topic. Of course, you've done your best to write for your audience, rather than at your audience, but sometimes you could make something clearer.

When you self-edit, take a break from your draft, if possible. Put it aside until the next morning or over the weekend. By getting away from it your mind will clear and you'll have a fresh look at your work. Of course, you'll have to plan ahead to give yourself the extra time.

Being Edited

Your work should be edited by someone else. If possible, find someone who is in the audience you have targeted for your message, or someone who is familiar with the audience. Be sure to tell your editor who the targeted audience is and the objective for your message. Make sure your editor knows what you expect him to do: edit for technical accuracy, clarity, conciseness, or all of them.

When your work has been edited, don't get defensive at the comments. Even professional writers have their work edited. Consider all the comments, but you don't have to accept them. Make sure you can justify your decision to accept or reject the comment.

Editing Others

When you edit someone else's work, be sure to ask who her audience is and her objective. Then make sure what kind of editing she wants you to do: that is, looking at the overall structure or just checking for misspelled words or all of the editing tasks. Be kind with the tone of your comments, and praise as well as point out mistakes.

EDITING SKILLS

Editing is the process of checking written documents for accuracy, completeness, and clarity, among other things. The steps to follow are the same order as for. writing the document. Start with checking the overall structure of the message and work down to the microcosm of words and punctuation. Editing is different from proofreading. Editing is more concerned with content and clarity than with correct spelling. Proofreading is part of editing, both may be done by the same person or by separate people.

Most editing is done on "hard copy," which is a printout of the document. The margins should be wider than normal (30 mm [1.25 in.] or more on each side), and the text must be double-spaced. Documents can also be edited on-screen, although that is different from the approach presented in this chapter.

Overall Structure

Before beginning the sentence-by-sentence editing, read the entire document for overall structure. Check for completeness and logical flow. You may need to change sections around, or delete entire sections, or add a new section. Try not to worry about the individual words at this point. Of course, you want to check how well the document met the communication principles:

- Is the topic appropriate and presented at the correct level of detail?
- Is the audience analysis valid and the message appropriate for them?
- Is the objective appropriate and has it been met?

Sometimes as you write the first draft, your original thoughts on the TAO for your message will change or be refined as the document is written. In the editing process, make sure the message is consistently written for the new TAO.

Paragraphs, Sentences, Words, Punctuation

When you're satisfied with the overall structure of the document, it's time to edit paragraphs and sentences. You'll need to work with tools called copyediting marks (Table 3).

Table 3. Copyediting Marks

Editing mark	Purpose
∦ydrology	Use lowercase
hydrology	Capitalize
hydology a science	Add letter or word
hydroloŏgy is is a science	Delete letter or word
hydrologys a science	Add apostrophe (or quote mark)
hydrology which is a science	Add comma
hydrology isa science	Add space
hydrolo gy is a science	Close space
hydrology a is science	Switch letter or word position
Hydrology is a science	Add period
Hydrology is a science. Hydrology	Start a new paragraph

You don't have to use these particular marks; others are used. But your organization should be consistent with those you do use.

When you edit, you want to fine-tune the document to meet the standards established in this book for paragraphs, sentences, words, phrases, and punctuation. The following paragraph is an example of editing:

Critical water system components are those vulnerable to failure because of disaster hazards. The goal of a water utility is to meet priority demand which is the minimum needed to maintain public health and safety. It is important to note that the failing of system components will reduce the ability of a utility to meet the goals. Identifying critical components is an important step in making a water system less vulnerable to disasters. The best way to approach identifying critical components is to assume a disaster scenario. Different types of disasters will affect components differently. Focus on the components that are interrelated with other components that would make the entire system inoperative. These are the most critical components. Assume the component is out of operation and then see how this affects the rest of the system. Repeat the process with other disaster scenarios. There are computer models you can use to simulate the loss.

STYLE SHEETS

Style sheets or style guides list document standards for an organization. Style sheets promote consistency and accuracy. The following items should be included:

- Proper use of the company name and logo
- Proper spelling of names of company employees and products
- Business letter, memo, and fax format
- Type and size of fonts to use
- Commonly used units of measure and how they're noted

- Approved abbreviations
- Footer and header style
- Copyediting marks

SUMMARY

Editing is necessary to achieve high quality written communications. Unfortunately, editing isn't done very often, or done well. Once you know that editing is applying the TAO communication principles, and you have a few guidelines and rules, then editing will be an easier task.

Chapter 12

ILLUSTRATIONS AND PAGE DESIGN

In previous chapters I've often mentioned that writing should be interesting, and suggested using examples and strong writing. Another way to make documents interesting is with illustrations and good page design. As with any good design, whether for a bridge or a building or a document, appearance is important. Not as important as content or structure, but it is the first thing noticed.

And you know what they say about first impressions.

Many excellent books are devoted to the subject of illustrations and page design. The intention here is to present basic guidelines.

ILLUSTRATIONS

> A picture is worth a thousand words.

Such a good saying that has been around for a while shouldn't be messed with, but perhaps it might be more accurate as: "A picture *can* be worth a thousand words." Well, as long as we're monkeying around with good sayings, let's change it to: "A *good* picture can be worth a thousand words."

How long is a thousand words anyway? About four double-spaced pages. You can say a lot in that space; for example, the Gettysburg Address was less than two pages. That's why a *good* picture *can be* worth a thousand words. What picture could be substituted for the Gettysburg Address? What makes a good picture?

Illustrations help the audience understand the message, and also break up pages of solid text. The rules for producing good illustrations are the same for communication in any form. The TAO communication principles apply, as does reducing noise.

Before developing an illustration, determine how the document will be printed. For example, we shouldn't produce a four-color drawing or use color photos if the document will be printed in black and white. Colors don't always translate clearly into grays or black-and-white. You've probably seen this happen when a nice graph that uses colors to show the different variables is photocopied in black-and-white. The colors are often indistinguishable. We also need to know the page size and space available for illustrations; they need to be readable at that final printed size.

Next, specific types of illustrations will be discussed in more detail.

Graphics

Graphics present concepts or results or prototypes. They can be graphs, drawings, flowcharts, or any other primarily visual representation. Graphics should be immediately, or at least quickly, understandable. For example, Figures 1 and 2 (pages 2-3) present time study results on a page from a daily calendar. Nearly everyone is familiar with such calendars, which should increase recall more than a tabular presentation of percentages.

The concept of chunking, presenting four to seven chunks of information at one time, applies to graphics. Figure 3 (page 11) of the RUN communication model has four elements: the two parties involved, the direction of understanding flow, and the noise that might interfere. Figures 6 and 7 (page 22) are examples of graphics that present concepts, in this case, the concept of overlapping frames of reference.

Graphs should not be skewed so the reader draws a wrong conclusion. An exaggerated axis scale often causes this problem. In Figure 17, for example, the graph on the left uses a y-axis scale that exaggerates a relationship which isn't significant. A more natural scale on the graph on the right shows the true relationship.

Tables

Tables are illustrations that organize data or knowledge. Tables can be set up in many ways, but they must be clear and concise.

- Organize the table to show the important points you want to make.
- Use dividing lines only between the titles, headings, and the data. Lines between each row and column are optional.
- Round off numbers to two significant places. For example: 86% rather than 86.42%.
- Be consistent with design in each document.
- Put units in headings rather than in cells.
- Put "not applicable" or a dash in cells without data.

Many references are available that show good table construction. Refer especially to Zimmerman and Clark (1987) and McCuen et al. (1993) for specifics.

Figure 17. The Effect of Scale

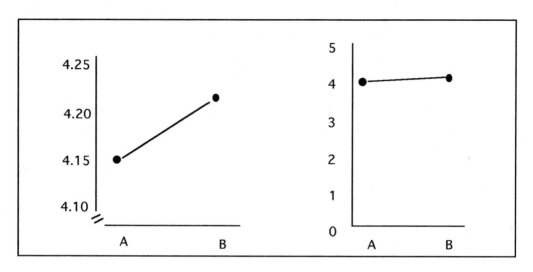

Photographs

Photos require more planning than just pointing and shooting. Many good photography references are also available. Guidelines for photos are as follows:

- Decide if a photo or line drawing will better show the detail you need.
- Tell a story with the photo.
- Frame the subject with adjacent objects to show scale and depth.
- Vary angle and position.
- Use the right film, that is, black-and-white, slide, or color prints.
- Take several shots at different angles and exposures.

PAGE DESIGN

You already know poor page design when you see it. It's noisy, confusing, cluttered, often illegible. Here are a few tips to improve the appearance of documents.

Typography

Typography is the arrangement and appearance of print. Here are some basics:

Font. The font or typeface should be easy to read. For most uses of long stretches of text, use a serif font (Figure 18). Serif fonts have extensions on the tips of the letters. The serif fonts are easier to read over long passages of text probably because the serifs more effectively tie the letters together into words.

Figure 18. Serif and Sans Serif Fonts

> This is a sans serif font.
> **This is a serif font.**

Use only one or two fonts in a document. For example, in this book I used a serif font (Times) for the main body of text, and a sans serif font (Geneva) for the text in boxes and figures.

Most serif fonts are also proportional. Fonts that are not proportional, such as Courier, give equal spacing to each letter. Non-proportional fonts are difficult to read and should not be used for most documents.

Size. Type that is too small or too large is difficult to read. Most documents use 9-12 point size, depending on the font.

Caps and lowercase. Engineers are used to reading all caps (capital letters) because most engineering plans use them. However, all caps are difficult to read. The theory is that the eye and brain recognize words by their shape as well as the letters in them as shown in Figure 19. Do not use all caps in written documents except for headings.

Figure 19. Word Shape

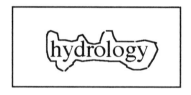

Margins and Justification

Use adequate margins, at least an inch on all sides. Many publications today are using left-only justification (right margin is ragged). Full justification often causes unequal word spacing, which is difficult to read and unattractive.

Headings

Be consistent with levels; they help the reader understand the levels of knowledge you're presenting. Headings also help break up the page and give the reader places to pause.

Use one font case (bold, italics, and underlining) for headings or emphasis, not two at once, or all.

White Space and Illustration Layout

Avoid a busy page. Leave plenty of white space (parts of the page that have nothing printed on them) for the eye to rest. Use boxes, sidebars (related information such as case studies) or quotes to make an interesting page.

Printer Quality

With the price of laser or equivalent printers coming down, organizations should have no excuse not to print high quality documents. Get one with at least 300 dpi (dots per inch), 600 is even better and not that much more expensive. Professional electronic printers can be as high as 2,400 dpi.

SUMMARY

This chapter is a brief introduction into the theories and applications of visual communication. Good illustrations help readers understand your message. Follow a few simple guidelines to make sure your illustrations are clear and not confusing. Illustrations and good page design help documents look appealing and interesting.

Okay, now you're overwhelmed by all the rules and guidelines for written messages. It is a lot to keep in mind, but with practice (there's that word again) you will become proficient. Use this section as a refresher and as a reference for a particular problem.

Enough on written messages; on to the spoken word.

Part III

SPOKEN AND INTERPERSONAL COMMUNICATION

Chapter 13

BASICS OF SPOKEN COMMUNICATION

A recent poll asked people to list their fears. The number one fear was speaking in public—ahead of flying, crime, snakes, and failing a test.

Why are we so afraid of speaking? Because everyone's attention is on us? The fear of having nothing to say? Or saying something wrong? That we'll bore our audience to tears? All of these reasons are probably responsible for the fear.

The next chapters present guidelines for preparing and giving spoken messages, from formal presentations to phone calls. Nonverbal communication, important for spoken messages, will also be discussed. And, we'll learn how to use the fear of public speaking to our advantage.

Remember, excellent communication skills can be learned. This most certainly applies to speaking and listening.

WHEN TO USE SPOKEN COMMUNICATION

Speaking is a more natural method of communication. It's one of the first things we learn as a child. A previous chapter already mentioned the theory that our brains are wired to understand and learn spoken language just by hearing it.

Spoken communication is more personal. It's often a faster way of reaching group consensus, or making decisions. Spoken messages are good for clarifying written messages, as research for written messages, or for putting faces and voices with message senders and receivers.

But in some ways spoken communication is less precise, mostly because we usually speak with less preparation than we spend writing. Presenting large amounts of knowledge orally is more difficult than with writing. Spoken messages offer no permanent record, unless they are taped.

Spoken and written messages often work together. Phone calls are often followed up with letters. Large reports are often formally presented with oral summaries. Meetings are documented with minutes.

First, let's see how TAO principles apply to spoken messages.

TOPIC, AUDIENCE, AND OBJECTIVE CONSIDERATIONS

Of course, our TAO principles apply to spoken messages. By using the principles you will be able to speak with ease and keep the audience interested. And they will understand and remember your message.

Topic

Remember to be an expert. Those words of advice will do a lot in making you a successful speaker. Why? Because you won't have to worry about what to say. You have facts on the tip of your tongue. Your audience will accept your message and accept you as messenger.

Speaking, as opposed to writing, requires you to think on your feet. The relaxed and confident speaker doesn't have to grope for answers to questions. The key to "on-your-feet-thinking" is preparation, which simply means becoming an expert. Refer to the chapter on topic for advice on becoming an expert.

Audience

Experts, with their knowledge sorted into levels of detail, speak to the audience at the appropriate level to achieve understanding. Experts don't talk down to the audience in a condescending manner. They don't say, "Well, you probably won't understand this, but ..." Experts don't roll their eyes at what could be considered a dumb question (an example of nonverbal communication, *bad* nonverbal communication).

Analyzing an audience is largely the same for spoken messages as for written messages. Consider their existing knowledge of the topic and their interest in the topic. Refer to the chapter on Audience for other audience considerations.

Objective

Of the four communication objectives we offered in a previous chapter, three apply mostly to spoken messages: Increase knowledge, persuade, and instruct. The fourth—document—rarely applies to spoken messages.

To increase knowledge with spoken messages, keep in mind that the message must be arranged carefully. By carefully, I mean logically and divided into chunks. With written messages, readers can go back and review the parts they don't understand. Of course, listeners can ask for clarification, but many questions will interrupt the flow of the message.

Persuasion with spoken messages is primarily the same for written messages. Overcoming any negatives with positives is the key. Instruction with spoken messages is also mostly the same for written messages. The advantage of spoken messages is that the instructor can see if the steps are understood before moving on.

We've seen how our TAO principles can apply to spoken messages in a general sense. Now, let's introduce the categories of spoken messages, which will be discussed in this part of the book.

CATEGORIES OF SPOKEN MESSAGES

For our purposes, consider the main categories of spoken messages as presentations, meetings, and interpersonal communication.

Presentations

Presentations are the most formal spoken communication. The primary sender is one person, and the audience has more than one person. The objectives can be to increase knowledge, persuade, or instruct.

Examples of increasing knowledge include reporting the results of a study or clarifying the facts of an issue. Persuasion examples include business proposals or providing evidence that one option is better than others. Instruction examples include training workshops or how-to seminars.

Meetings

Meetings differ from presentations because one person isn't sending messages to many receivers. Although, you've probably been in meetings where that was exactly the case.

The primary goal of meetings is to reach consensus on a course of action. Reaching a group decision is an exercise in problem-solving and is conducted as a series of communications. The objectives of these communications are primarily increasing knowledge and persuasion.

Interpersonal Communication

Interpersonal communication, for the purposes of this book, refers to one person talking to one other person. Interpersonal communication skills are increasingly important to managers because managers manage people.

Interpersonal communication can be for the purpose of increasing knowledge, persuasion, and instruction. Interpersonal communications are often used when resolving conflicts and giving and getting criticism. It is also the skill used in everyday conversation.

COMMON NOISE IN SPOKEN MESSAGES

Much of the noise that interfered with the understanding of written messages is the same for spoken messages. Those sources will be reviewed and new sources of noise that apply to spoken messages will be introduced.

Poor Logic

Listeners want to understand what you're saying. Give them all the help you can by structuring your messages logically. Go from broad to narrow. Give your points from most important to least important. Follow a procedure step-by-step. List events chronologically. Logical flow helps the listener tie things together into chunks.

Omission

More often than not, listeners will know when you've left out important knowledge, intentionally or not. They may be waiting for you to fill in the gap, or wonder if there's a reason for the void. Confusion can result and spoil the entire presentation. Make sure you've thought about your audience's needs before you speak. This will help eliminate omissions.

Redundancy

Redundancy will put off your audience, making them wish you'd move on (or move off the stage). However, summarizing at various points in a presentation is not being redundant. Summarizing is discussed in the next chapter.

Unclear Words or Jargon

Speak to your audience in terms they understand. Be concrete, not abstract; clear, not muddy. When we speak, as when we write, we should use strong verbs, specific details, and examples.

Poor Voice and Presentation quality

Reading a speech is the best way to put your audience to sleep. A stiff, non-conversational tone, or a voice that is too quiet or too loud or monotone will also interfere with your audience's understanding. Correct grammar when speaking is just as important as using correct grammar when writing. Correct pronunciation is as important as correct spelling. A few examples of commonly mispronounced words follow. These examples come from two excellent books on pronunciation by Elster (1988, 1990). Dictionaries normally list the preferred pronunciation first.

- **Data** (DAY-tuh, not DAT-uh)
- **Comparable** (KAHM-purr-uh-bull, not kuhm-PAIR-uh-bull or KAHM-pruh-bull)
- **Decibel** (DES-i-bell, not DES-i-bull)
- **Either** (EE-thur, not EYE-thur)
- **Mischievous** (MIS-chi-vus, not mis-CHEE-vi-us)
- **Vehicle** (VEE-i-kle, the h is silent)
- **Vice versa** (VY-suh VUR-suh, not VYS Vur-suh)

Poor Listening and Interpersonal Skills

Nothing is a barrier to success as a manager more than poor listening and interpersonal skills. You know when someone isn't listening, or doesn't care what you're saying. A temper that flares up at the least criticism is another barrier.

Poor Use of Humor

Humor is the best thing you can use when speaking. And the worst. A gentle, often self-effacing, form of humor that doesn't belittle anyone else is best. Especially forget about puns, and off-color or long jokes. How would you judge the story found in the sidebar?

Poor nonverbal communication

Moderation is the key. Don't be too stiff or too relaxed. Don't dress too casually or too formally, unless the situation demands. Don't stand in one place or run all over the room. Be attentive, but don't nod wide-eyed at every word. Don't nod "yes" when you're saying "no."

Our friend Nancy and her next door neighbor, Paula, had a running feud going over their pets. Nancy's dog, Ruffy, was always into Paula's yard digging around and tormenting Paula's cat, Muffy. Of course, Nancy maintained that Muffy was the one doing all the digging and tormenting.

Early one morning, Nancy noticed Ruffy playing with what looked like a dead cat in her yard. Sure enough, it was Muffy. Muffy was dead, and not a pretty sight. Nancy picked up the cat and hurried into the house. "Ruffy," Nancy said, "we're in trouble now. You've gone and killed Muffy."

Nancy put the cat into the bathtub and washed off the dirt and blood. She toweled off the body and blow dried it. Then she snuck over to Paula's and put poor Muffy on the doorstep. She hurried back home. "Maybe she'll think Muffy had a heart attack or something," she told Ruffy.

An hour later, Nancy's door bell rang. Paula was there, looking very distressed. Nancy sighed and opened the door. Paula said, "Oh, Nancy, I'm so upset. Muffy died a couple of days ago and I think I buried her alive."

SUMMARY

The TAO principles and RUN communication model apply to spoken messages as much as they do to written messages. This chapter introduced the three main categories of spoken messages—presentations, meetings, and interpersonal communication. Many of the sources of noise found in written messages also can be found in spoken messages. The next chapters show you how to eliminate the noise. And you'll be shown how to reduce (and use to your advantage) the anxiety of public speaking all of us suffer from.

Chapter 14

PRESENTATIONS

You've sat through hundreds of presentations by now. You know they can be agonizing, energizing, successful, interesting, boring, and anything in between. You can't avoid giving presentations, if you're an engineer or a manager. How would you like to be known as a good speaker, one who gets praised after a presentation? One who keeps the audience on the edge of their seats (at least awake)? One who wins that contract or convinces a board to choose the best alternative?

No magic is needed to transform the most reluctant speaker into one glowing with confidence. Just a few tips to consider when planning and making presentations will make you the type of presenter we all admire. Anyone can do it. You can do it. Your employees can do it.

This chapter will present those few things, from organizing the presentation, to using visuals, to jazzing up your presentations, to understanding and using nonverbal communication. But first, we'll start by doing something about the fear we all have for public speaking.

HEALTHFUL VS. PARALYZING FEAR

Even after all those years on the Tonight Show, Johnny Carson admitted he fought stage fright. Of course, paralyzing fear is different from healthful fear. Paralyzing fear causes a person to freeze, the mind to go blank. Healthful fear, on the other hand, can help you in many ways. Healthful fear:

- Makes you alert
- Keeps you focused
- Gives you energy
- Drives you to prepare and practice
- Forces you to make your presentation interesting

So instead of "We have nothing to fear but fear itself" the saying should be "We have nothing to fear but paralyzing fear." We don't even have to fear fear, as long as it's healthful fear.

ORGANIZE THE PRESENTATION

The following are guidelines for organizing the typical presentation.

Answer TAO Questions

As discussed in the previous chapter as well as in previous sections of the book, the first step in planning a message is to answer these three questions:

- What is the topic?
- Who is the audience?
- What is the objective?

By now, you should know how to answer those questions; refer to the appropriate chapter for more details.

Arrange the Major Points

Jot down the major points you want to cover. Arrange them into an order that makes sense to your audience. That is, from broad to narrow, step-by-step, or chronologically. Other basics of arranging the major points include:

Start effectively. Get the audience involved right away. Start with an example they can relate to, or with an interesting visual. Make them a partner in the presentation by appealing to their interests. Tell the audience what you're going to speak about by listing the main points.

Summarize occasionally. When you finish a part of your presentation, summarize the main points before moving on.

Close effectively. An effective closing ties things together. Highlight the two to four main points you want the audience to remember, even if they don't remember anything else you've said.

Fit the Presentation into Time Allotted

Nothing is worse than a presentation that drags on past the time allowed. A presentation that is too short is only slightly better. With careful planning it can be prepared exactly to fit. Put estimated times next to your major points that you arranged from the previous step. Adjust them until you've reached the allotted time. Be sure to leave time for questions if they are to be allowed.

VISUALS AIDS AS MEMORY AIDS

Visual aids help an audience understand a message. They break up long stretches of speech, just as illustrations break up pages of text, and they illustrate concepts and results. But visual aids serve a more important function—they act as memory aids for the speaker. If visual aids are prepared correctly, speakers shouldn't have to use any other notes. By not using notes, the speaker's tone is more conversational, and she is more in touch with her audience.

Of course, the visual aids a speaker can use depends on the facility and equipment available. In general, visual aids need to be very simple and clear. They need to be seen by everyone in the room, including those in the back row. They need to be quickly understood, because they are usually shown for only a few seconds. The amount of text should be limited to a few lines of few words.

Next, guidelines for specific visual aids will be presented.

Overhead Transparencies

Overhead transparencies can be used for text as well as drawings. Most meeting facilities will have overhead projectors. Be sure to arrange them so that you won't have to do any backtracking. Digging around for previous transparencies can interrupt the flow of the presentation.

Transparencies can be written on during the presentation, which is a good way to emphasize a specific point. The "uncover" method (Figure 20) is a good way to keep the audience focused on what you're saying. To use this method simply cover the transparency with a piece of paper and pull it down as you talk about each point.

Figure 20. The Uncover Method for Transparencies

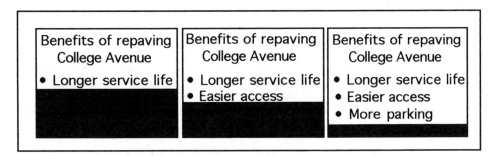

Another way to use overhead projectors is with a computer. A notebook computer, with all the visuals loaded onto the hard drive, can be connected to a LCD display. The display sits on the projector. This system works best with a high quality projector with a very bright bulb; projectors for this purpose are available.

Make sure you check the projection behind you occasionally. Often the image ends up on the ceiling or gets out of focus. Also, make sure that the image isn't too low on the wall or screen to be seen. This will happen if your transparency is too long; you might want to keep the information on the upper two thirds or so of each transparency.

Flip Charts and Marking Boards

When using flip charts for presentations, be sure they can be seen from every seat. Flip charts are useful for smaller group presentations and they can be prepared in advance or can be done during the presentation. Use large block letters.

Boards refer to chalk boards or white boards for use with markers. They are limiting, because of size. But they are good for writing down as you go, or making quick sketches in response to questions. They are used mostly for informal presentations and small groups.

Slides

Slide shows work well in formal presentations. They are especially good for illustrating examples. They can also be used to present the points of your presentations, similar to overheads (of course, the uncover method can't be used). Many software packages are available to produce the slides. See the previous chapter's section on photos for advice on taking good pictures to be used with slide presentations. Be sure the room is set up for slides (a large blank wall or screen, lighting that can be dimmed).

Video and Multimedia

Video is an excellent way to show examples; of course, the room must be set up for video. A television can only be seen from a limited distance, if a projection system isn't available. Of course, video production can be expensive (around $1,000 per minute of finished tape), but nothing can illustrate and hold attention better than a professional video.

Multimedia refers to a computer-based method of presenting text, graphics, animation, sounds, and video. The ultimate in visual aids, multimedia systems are now available for relatively low costs, and the software available to produce multimedia is becoming easy to use.

Exhibits

Other visual aids can be the actual examples of what you're talking about: a flowmeter, a computer printout, a pavement core. Make sure they can be seen by everyone. If the exhibits are to be handed around for inspection, then it's best if the group is small, otherwise the last person will get it when you're on another topic.

PRESENTATION EXAMPLE

The following example illustrates the process of organizing presentations.

Topic: Repaving of College Avenue.

Audience: Business owners along affected area. Probably fifty in attendance.

Objective: To persuade them the selected paving plan and schedule will create the minimum disruption to their businesses. To engender goodwill and cooperation between the city and the business owners.

Time: Sixty minutes: 30 for presentation, 30 for questions.

Main point	Visual aid	Min
Introduction, thank them for previous participation, assure them their input was used in selecting best alternative	—	2
Review alternatives	Overhead list	3
Positive and negative features of each rejected alternative	Diagrams, maps	5
Selected alternative (concrete-Plan C)	Diagrams, maps	3
Reasons . 1. Service life longer 2. Easier temporary access 3. More parking	Overhead list of the three reasons	2
Construction techniques and schedule	Slides, overheads	3
How they can help during construction, traffic routing	Overhead list, video of similar construction	7
Questions	As needed	30 [55 total]

HANDOUTS

Handouts are written copies of a presentation or a summary of a presentation. They can also simply be copies of the transparencies. They can be handed out before you begin or after you've finished. Most often, it's best to hand them out after the talk. This way your audience will be focused on what you say rather than leafing through the handout. Inform the audience before you begin that they don't need to write down everything you say, since they will be getting the notes after your presentation.

PRACTICE

Practice is critical to becoming a good presenter. Take every opportunity you have to stand in front of people and speak. You'll also need to practice the individual presentation. You can do it out loud to yourself or in front of coworkers, or to yourself.

Practicing will help you see that you've covered all the points, allows you to put in good transitions from one part of the presentation to the next, and gets you comfortable using your visual aids.

However, you don't want your presentation to sound stiff, as if you've memorized it. This can happen if you practice too much. Remember to keep your tone conversational.

SUMMARY

The most important thing to remember is that anyone can be an excellent and comfortable speaker. Giving good presentations is easy if you follow the communication principles and practice a few professional techniques.

Be relaxed and enjoy yourself; your audience will do the same.

Chapter 15

MEETINGS

> "Let's set up a meeting to discuss that."
>
> Quote heard across the land, millions of times a day.

You've been in bad meetings and good meetings. Bad meetings waste time. Good meetings start with a purpose and accomplish it. Unfortunately, bad meetings outnumber good meetings 18.6 to 1. Roughly.

Meetings are firmly entrenched into our corporate routine. And that isn't all bad. Meetings are necessary in a participatory style of management. The problem is that meetings aren't always the best way to get participation.

Everyone complains about meetings, but nobody seems to do much about making good meetings the norm. Yet we should know how to make meetings run better. Many books have been written on management and they all have a chapter on meetings. We've heard about setting an agenda, about keeping the discussion on the topic, about keeping the meeting short. These steps to good meetings seem to be easy enough; why doesn't everyone use them? The old saying about leading a horse to water may apply.

Most meetings fail because they are not approached from any methodology or consistent plan of attack. This chapter presents a plan that can easily make meetings more productive. But don't wait for someone else to put it into action; you have to.

APPLYING COMMUNICATION PRINCIPLES

Think of meetings as a series of communication events. That way we can apply our TAO communication principles as described in the following paragraphs.

Agenda Items Are Communication Topics

Having an agenda set in advance of the meeting allows the participants to prepare. Just as we prepare for any communication event, we need to become experts in the topic. Knowing the topic (agenda item) also prevents the meeting from wandering into other areas.

Meeting Participants Are the Audience

As you know by now, to communicate well we need to know our audience. In the case of meetings, the audience will be the participants. If we know who the participants are, we can tailor what we're going to communicate. If you're in charge of the meeting, be sure to include a list of the participants when you send out the agenda. If you're a participant in the meeting, be sure to find out who the other participants are.

Agenda Item Goals Are Communication Objectives

Each agenda item should have a specific goal. The goals could be to bring everyone up to speed on a project, or to select a course of action. The goals provide you with objectives for your messages. For example, if you're supposed to discuss the status of a project, the corresponding communication objective is to increase knowledge. If the goal is to select from several options, and you prefer one of the options, then your communication objective is to persuade.

Because meetings are generally too long, concise messages must be the rule rather than the exception. And as we've seen, concise messages require a bit of work. Boil down your expertise on the topic to a few sentences. Prepare an illuminating graph.

MEETING NOISE

You'll no doubt recognize many of the following sources of noise. Some of the sources were identified by Walton (1989).

Interruptions

You've been to meetings where one participant feels he is so important that he has to have his phone calls transferred to the room or messages delivered instantly. He is usually late for the meeting, constantly fidgets and checks his watch, and then rushes out before the meeting is finished.

Negativity

There's always one person who shoots down every idea not her own. She dwells on minutia and has figured out why something won't work. Frequently she is wrong because she hasn't grasped the concept of the idea, which happens because she doesn't listen well.

Domination

He dominates not with whips and chains, but with an oral assault. He often speaks too loudly, and always has something to say even when his message is irrelevant. And the more irrelevant the louder he gets, as if enough decibels will convince everyone he knows what he's talking about. The chair of the meeting needs to control him. If this person is the chair, the other participants must mutiny.

Defensiveness

The defensive person takes each criticism or question as a personal attack. As she defends her position her face flushes and her voice quivers. She gets frustrated and tongue-tied, and waits for a chance to jump her perceived attackers' ideas.

Silence

The quiet type sits and studies the agenda. He often takes word-for-word notes, even if he isn't the appointed minutes-taker. He may have something to say, but lacks the confidence to jump in or lets his chance go by as he mentally rehearses what he wants to say.

Rambling

Those who ramble rarely get to the point and sometimes admit they've forgotten what the point was to begin with. Their discourse tends to take them far away from the agenda item.

Politics

Office politics will happen in meetings—turf building, playing "yes" person, coalition forming, grandstanding, and false praise or self praise. Of course, those who are more worried about playing politics than concentrating on the agenda item rarely have much of value to contribute.

Stories and Jokes

Unfortunately, we've all met The Story Teller. Everything reminds him of an experience he had, often overseas. He'll tell the same story over and over, until you start to count the number of times you've heard it. The Jokester has in her mental filing cabinet 3,000 jokes, one [un]suitable for every discussion.

Coffee and Pastry

The hungry meeting participant can't concentrate on the discussion because he's too busy selecting from the pastry tray. He's a frustrated waiter too, and would rather be pouring coffee for everyone than contributing to the matters at hand.

Doodles and Yawns

You think the person hunched over her pad of yellow lined paper is busy taking notes, but actually she's creating amazing ink doodles. The only thing that interrupts the creation of art is her poorly stifled yawning.

ACCOMPLISHING MEETING GOALS

One of the best ways to assure the goals of the meeting are accomplished is to use problem-solving techniques. The following are the problem-solving steps applied to meetings:

1. *Ask the right question.* Make sure everyone in the meeting is discussing the same issue and understands the goal. For example, if an agenda item is to decide which method of storm detention to use, then don't list the item as a discussion of detention methods. The agenda item should be to reach that decision.

2. *Determine what method to use.* If we consider each agenda item a mini-communication event, then determine the objective of the agenda item. In other words will it be to increase knowledge or persuade or another objective? The objective will let you know how to approach the item. For example, to increase knowledge, you need to make sure those participants who have knowledge of the item give their input.

3. *List the data or knowledge you need to solve the problem.* What are the criteria needed to make a decision? By listing all the data or knowledge needed to solve a problem, you can be sure that they will be presented at the meeting. Otherwise, the goal can't be reached and another meeting will have to be set up.

4. *List the data or knowledge you already have.*

5. *Find the data or knowledge you need.*

6. *Solve the problem.* Make the decision or give the presentation.

7. *Evaluate the solution.* Summarize what the group decided or list the highlights of the presentation.

USABLE MINUTES

Taking, preparing, and distributing minutes is an example of documenting—one of the communication objectives. If you're taking minutes, the most important things to keep track of are action items and decisions. Action items are the items agreed to be completed by meeting participants. To make sure the minutes are accurate, during the meeting read the action items and decisions as you've noted them.

When you produce the minutes, list the action items and decisions directly beneath the agenda items. Other discussion is rarely necessary. If the agenda item is an update, then list the main points in short, bulleted or numbered sentences. Send out the minutes within a few days.

TAKING OVER (GENTLY)

Meetings usually are only as good as the chair, or leader, makes them. Bad meetings are never the intent of any chair, but sometimes chairs just do not follow the steps that make good meetings. If you're a participant in a meeting that isn't going well because of an ineffective chair, you need to help the chair without seeming like you're taking over or blaming the chair for wasting everyone's time.

For example, someone isn't participating who you feel has valuable input and the chair isn't prodding him into speaking. You could say to Jane, the chair, "As I'm sure you know, Jane, Steve knows a lot about that issue. I wouldn't mind if we got his side of the story." If a chair isn't summarizing the main points of a discussion, you could say, "Sorry, Jane, I'm a little confused. Could you summarize the main points?" Or you could summarize the points to see if you've (and the rest of the participants who are doodling or pouring coffee) got them correct.

TELEPHONE CONFERENCE CALLS

Conference calls are meetings that take place on the phone. They save the expense of the participants having to travel to a meeting place. Someday, everyone will have a video phone that will make such meetings easier, but for now, the conference call is limited to voice phone. Telephone companies or teleconferencing specialty companies can set up the call for you.

The keys to a successful phone conference are to send out an agenda beforehand and to have a system of input. The best system is to have the leader read down an alphabetical list of the participants and have each person give their input on the first agenda item. Let each know he or she has only a few seconds to speak. After each round the leader summarizes the discussion, then asks for clarification and further discussion. The leader goes down the list again until the agenda item goal is reached. Then the next agenda item is tackled.

SUMMARY

Meetings can be productive if a they are approached as communication events. Clearly define the agenda items and their goals. Reduce sources of noise that interfere with the understanding and productivity of the participants. Use problem-solving techniques to reach the goals of the agenda items.

Now that the meeting is over, go ahead and grab one of those pastries.

Chapter 16

INTERPERSONAL COMMUNICATION

Remember the first chapter of this book? Besides the phrase "excellent communication skills required," another phrase often seen in employment ads was mentioned: "must have good interpersonal skills" or "good people skills." So, what are good interpersonal or people skills?

As you may have anticipated, I feel interpersonal skills are primarily communication skills. The communication events involve two people or a small group of people, such as a team. The communication is primarily speaking and listening. We can apply our communication principles, model, and techniques to these events, just as we have for written messages and other spoken messages.

This chapter will look at several common interpersonal situations: conflict and criticism, conversation, phone calls, and job candidate interviews.

CONFLICT AND ANGER

Conflict is a noun and a verb (pronounced differently). Conflict's most benign definition is to differ in opinion, and "ain't nothing" wrong with that. The problem is that conflict can boil over into anger and arguments.

Anger is one of the noisiest sources of noise that can interfere with the communication of understanding. Reducing the chances for anger is your responsibility. Even if you're right (of course you're right). Even if you're not the one with the temper. Even if the other person deserves a good screaming at.

You're responsible for controlling your own anger. A few tips to help you do just that are:

- *Know what makes you angry.* Do certain topics, or viewpoints, or personality types set you off? Think about the times when you vented your anger at someone and figure out the real reason for your anger. Were you being defensive, or did the person hit a nerve that you try to protect from the world? If you know what makes you angry, then you can start your anger warning system in those situations.

- *Know when you're reaching your boiling point.* As you think about those times when your anger showed, try to remember the physiological and psychological changes that overtook your reason. Did you start to breath quickly and shallowly? Did your jaw clench, and maybe your fist? Did your mind race and cloud over? If you experienced these symptoms or others shortly before you exploded in a rage, then learn to use them to defuse the anger. Analyze them as they start to occur. This will take your mind off the cause of the anger. And, as with biofeedback techniques, you focus your energy on lessening the symptoms and thus the anger.

- *Detach yourself from the situation.* Detachment is also known as the out-of-body technique. Pretend that you're a third person mediating the argument. How does a mediator work? A mediator first tries to understand both points of view. You, as mediator, also must understand both points of view. Start with the other person's first. Repeat their point of view and ask if you've got it right. Ask the other person if they understand your point of view, and ask if there is any common ground. Agree to those things first. Then work on the conflicting viewpoints as calmly as possible.

- *Retreat.* As a last resort say: "Look, I'm not thinking too clearly now. Could we take a break to let me clear my head? I'd like to think about what you've said."

How can you control someone else's anger? First, don't provoke him to anger. We know what words can set other people off: "That's stupid." "Don't be ridiculous." And don't bring up old arguments that were never settled, or past mistakes the person may have made.

If the person is angry, try to defuse it. But not with humor! Or even with a smile. Take the person's anger seriously. In fact, the best way to cool another person's anger is to take the blame for their anger. Say: "I'm sorry I caused a misunderstanding here. I may have said something out of place."

If the other person's anger subsides, then get the discussion back to the facts of the situation. If the anger persists, retreat.

CRITICISM

Another valuable interpersonal skill, similar in many ways to dealing with anger, is getting and giving criticism. Getting criticism can be a painful experience. We usually try our best in whatever we do, and to hear that we could be doing something better often can be perceived as an attack on us personally.

But getting criticism actually helps us grow. We aren't saying that all criticism is correct. Sometimes your approach is the best. But on the other hand it may not be, and we all want to be better coworkers, bosses, or friends. So the first step is to try to fully understand the criticism. Get analytical rather than defensive. Controlling defensiveness is the same as controlling anger.

If the criticism is valid, then you can agree to it and ask for suggestions on how to improve. If you feel the criticism isn't valid, then present your case in factual terms. In other words, don't attack, but resort to good communication principles and techniques. Use persuasion and problem solving.

Giving criticism is also an exercise in good communication. Follow the TAO principles and RUN communication model. First, reduce the noise: don't jump on someone with a "Boy, did you screw up." Or even "You're wrong." Those phrases automatically set you up for a defensive reaction. Lead into the criticism gently. "I'm not sure about what you did here, maybe you could help me understand."

Then, as an expert, you should present facts for your criticism, not just because that's what you feel is best. Remain an open-minded listener if the other person disagrees. Use problem-solving techniques. Reach a compromise, if possible. Bring in a third person to mediate.

THE ART OF CONVERSATION

Conversation is everyday talking and listening. It can be small talk or the discussion of important issues. It is about business, and hobbies, and family. About life.

Conversation is important because it's how we most often interact with our fellow human beings. And those at the managerial level have to do it a lot. Remember, you're managing people. Part of managing people is not only dealing with them on a business level, but on a personal level.

So what makes a good conversationalist? Quite simply, it's not about talking at all. It's about listening. The art of conversation then is the art of listening. And the only technique in the art of listening to learn is: ask questions.

Conversation is that simple. It works. Even the shyest person in the world who thinks he or she has nothing to say, can ask a question. The other person will do the talking, and all you have to do is listen. And ask another question.

Once the conversation is started, asking questions does something else. To ask questions, you have to be listening attentively. And when you listen attentively, the other person knows that you are, and you are seen as a great conversationalist. And wonderful person.

Ask questions that can't be answered "yes" or "no." Remember the five "W's and an H": who, what, when, where, why, and how.

Asking questions also prevents too many conversation killers, that is, sentences that start with "I." You know when that happens. Say you are talking about your weekend ski trip. The other person listens until he can jump in with: "I went skiing in the French Alps once."

"Oh?" you say. "That's great. Anyway, the snow was really excellent on Saturday—"

"I like to ski on just about two inches of powder," he jumps in again. "I hate to ski on ice, but too much powder is hard on my knees."

About this time you give up and ask if his knees were injured by people kicking him for being a poor conversationalist.

If the other person is a good conversationalist as well, she will get into the conversation by asking you questions. You can of course get into the conversation by adding your viewpoint or experience, but don't leave the other person dangling. Finish your part of the dialogue by asking a question.

If the other person isn't letting you into the conversation, and you've asked all the questions you can think of, then stop asking questions. In fact, don't say anything. The other person will be flustered. He may even ask you a question. If not, and he launches into another story about the French Alps, then you may have to excuse yourself politely.

TELEPHONE CALLS

You probably spend a lot of time on the phone. Most people rate phone calls just below meetings as an irritant. But, as with meetings, a lot *can* get done over the phone. Using the phone well doesn't require a lot of special communication techniques over and above the ones already given. But because the telephone has its own characteristics, here are a few tips:

- Assume the other person is very busy. When you call someone, you don't know what they are in the middle of. You should say who you are and what you're calling about right away. If your call might go more than two minutes, ask if they have the time.
- You don't have to answer your phone if you're busy or if you have someone in your office. Have your calls forwarded or answered by a machine or voice mail, rather than have someone sit while you talk on

the phone. You wouldn't let someone barge into your office and interrupt a conversation; phone calls are the same thing. Of course, if you're trying to get rid of the person in your office, a phone call might be a diplomatic way. ("You will excuse me, won't you? I've been waiting for this call all week.")

- Avoid the use of a second line that will interrupt your first call. Have someone else or voice mail answer the second call.
- Be polite, use good spoken language, and don't put another person in a bad light. Here are some examples of poor phone etiquette:
  "I have no idea what you're talking about."
  "I dunno."
  "She's not in yet; she's late as usual."
- To avoid playing telephone tag, return calls promptly. Leave a time for the person to call back.

RECOGNIZING GOOD COMMUNICATION SKILLS

As a manager you will be interviewing job candidates. And you will want to find out how well they communicate. Ask them how they would prepare for a presentation to a city council or a client. Ask them to bring some of the reports or letters they've written, or have them submit samples with their resume.

You can find out about their interpersonal skills during the interview: how they answer questions, and if they ask questions. You could also ask them how they would respond to situations of conflict or anger.

SUMMARY

This book ends with a chapter on interpersonal communications skills, or how to get along with people. It's actually the most important communication skill you'll need, not only in your career, but in all aspects of life.

BIBLIOGRAPHY

Blake, Gary, and Bly, Robert W. 1991. *The Elements of Business Writing*. Collier Books, New York, NY.

Carnegie, Dale. 1962. *The Quick and Easy Way To Effective Speaking*. Pocket Books, New York, NY.

Elster, Charles H. 1988. *There is No Zoo in Zoology, and Other Beastly Mispronunciations: An Opinionated Guide for the Well-Spoken*. Collier Books, New York, NY.

Elster, Charles H. 1990. *Is there a Cow in Moscow? More Beastly Mispronunciations and Sound Advice: Another Opinionated Guide for the Well-Spoken*. Collier Books, New York, NY.

Flesch, Rudolf. 1960. *How to Write, Speak, and Think More Effectively*. Signet, New York, NY.

Gordon, Karen E. 1984. *The Transitive Vampire, A Handbook of Grammar for the Innocent, the Eager, and the Doomed*. Times Books, New York, NY.

McCuen, Richard H., Johnson, Peggy A., and Davis, Cynthia. 1993. *Dynamic Communication for Engineers*. American Society of Civil Engineers, New York, NY.

Munter, Mary. 1992. *Guide to Managerial Communication, Third Edition*. Prentice Hall, Englewood Cliffs, NJ.

National Academy of Engineering. 1991. *Engineering as a Social Enterprise*. National Academy Press, Washington, DC.

Strunk, William Jr., and White, E.B. 1979. *The Elements of Style.* Macmillan Publishing Co., New York, NY.

Walton, Donald. 1989. *Are You Communicating? You Can't Manage Without It.* McGraw-Hill Publishing Company, New York, NY.

Whitman, Marina v.N. 1991. "Business, Consumers, and Society-at-Large: New Demands and Expectations." *Engineering as a Social Enterprise.* National Academy Press, Washington, DC. 41-57.

Zimmerman, Donald E., and Clark, David G. 1987.*The Random House Guide to Technical and Scientific Communication.* Random House, New York, NY.

INDEX

110